Amazing AND CURIOUS

RAILWAY TALES

COLIN G. MAGGS

Amazing

AND

CURIOUS

RAILWAY
TALES

The
History
Press

Cover illustrations: Adam Bignell, Unsplash.

First published 2021

The History Press
97 St George's Place, Cheltenham,
Gloucestershire, GL50 3QB
www.thehistorypress.co.uk

British Library Cataloguing in Publication Data.
A catalogue record for this book is available from the British Library.

ISBN 978 0 7509 9431 6

Typesetting and origination by The History Press
Printed and bound by Imak, Turkey

CONTENTS

Introduction	7
Note to the Reader	7
1 Stations	9
2 Travelling by Train	29
3 Locomotives	59
4 Workforce	97
5 Track	123
6 Accidents	147
7 Rolling Stock	155
8 Miscellany	170
Index	222

INTRODUCTION

Railways are fun. Railways are intriguing and mysterious – it seems incredible that a narrow steel wheel can remain on a narrow rail without falling off, the flange keeping it in place being so slender.

Railways are curious – the unexpected can happen. Mail bags can be picked up and dropped without the train stopping; a locomotive's tender can be refilled with water while on the move; just part of a train can stop at a station while the rest speeds through.

It is difficult to accept that a few British railways actually used the wind to propel their trains, while in 1930 a race was held from London to Dover between a pigeon and an express train.

Railways are full of unexpected surprises: a locomotive once helped a ship in distress. Read on and you will discover the details of that and more absorbing facts.

NOTE TO THE READER

Train times in this book are those given in official timetables: the twelve-hour clock being used previous to June 1963 and the twenty-four-hour clock subsequently. To avoid confusion, 'Up' and 'Down' are capitalised when used for direction, with lower case for gradients.

Thanks are due to Colin Roberts for checking and improving the text.

1

STATIONS

A TIDAL STATION

It sounds like an April Fools' Day joke, but it is actually true that Bristol Temple Meads station rises and falls 2mm with the tide twice daily.

The station is between the Floating Harbour and the River Avon: the Floating Harbour is so-called because the water level is governed by locks and weirs to keep it at a constant level so ships no longer topple over when the tide goes out, while the River Avon is tidal. The ebb and flow of the water causes the station to rise and fall correspondingly.

The Great Western Railway station at Dartmouth was also tidal but more curious for the fact that it had no rails and no trains. The reason was that they terminated on the opposite bank of the River Dart at Kingswear, which was linked to Dartmouth station by a GWR ferry. Curiously, due to the Royal Naval College traffic, the station master at Dartmouth was of a higher grade than his colleague at Kingswear, despite having no trains.

A SINKING STATION

There was so much coal in Fife, some of it below the railway, and Thornton station became affected by subsidence. It sank so much that a new station was built. This also sank and had to be replaced by a third.

IN THREE COUNTIES

Dovey Junction station was in Montgomeryshire, the station master's house in Merionethshire and a distant signal in Cardiganshire.

A SCHOOL PREVENTS
A STATION BEING BUILT

When the Great Western Railway was planned, Eton College was alarmed by the fact that its pupils would have easy access to the evils of London. It was unable to avert the line being built through Slough on the opposite bank of the Thames, but was able to prevent a station being erected within 3 miles of the school. This included Slough, so the GWR cunningly rented part of a public house adjacent to the railway as a booking office. On 1 June 1838 the college appealed to the court for an injunction to prevent trains stopping at Slough, but the appeal was rejected.

A few weeks later Eton College ordered special trains to take its pupils to London to see the coronation of Queen Victoria!

BUILDINGS RECYCLED AS STATIONS

Slough was not the only example of railways recycling buildings. In its early years, the Stockton & Darlington Railway also used local inns economically as booking offices. Similarly, the station at Bourne, Lincolnshire, was Red Hall, a recycled mansion; that at

Hartlepool used the poop of a Dutch sailing ship, while Norwich utilised the theatre buildings of a pleasure garden.

The Liverpool & Manchester did not go to the expense of intermediate stations; trains were merely stopped at predetermined places, often level crossings, by a railway policeman holding a red flag, or red lamp, passengers climbing up into the carriages as they would have done at a coaching inn.

HAVING A WHALE OF A GOOD TIME

It is said that Pevensey Bay Halt near Eastbourne was opened to cater for the crowds that travelled from London and elsewhere to view a whale washed up on the beach.

PLATFORM REGULATIONS
HAVE GONE OFF THE RAILS

In 2015 a gentleman was due to meet his wife at Dundee station. When he requested a platform ticket, the Scotrail employee said they were no longer available. The wife-greeter explained that he wished to carry her bag, but was told: 'You can wait by the barrier.'

The employee offered to sell him a ticket to the nearest station for £3.50 – and a return was necessary so he could get back again. With his railcard this was reduced to £2.50, so he paid, had a joyful reunion with his wife and was able to carry her bags. He believed this instance to be bureaucracy out of control.

Apparently this directive defied the Department for Transport rules, which state that, unless circumstances are exceptional, non-travellers must be allowed access to platforms. The station operator may charge for a platform ticket, but not if a disabled person is involved.

THE NARROWEST WAITING ROOM?

One of the narrowest waiting rooms could be found on the island platform of the Midland Railway's West Hampstead station: it was only 4ft 3in wide.

RED LIGHT FOR STATION'S POPPY DISPLAY

In 2015 dozens of giant poppies were attached to pillars running the length of the platform at Surbiton railway station by the bosses of South West Trains. However, these tributes to fallen soldiers were removed within forty-eight hours after concerns had been raised that train drivers might mistake the poppies for red lights.

One commuter commented: 'I saw the poppies at the weekend and thought how lovely they were – they really brightened up the station. It's such a shame they have now been removed; it's crazy really. If a train driver could mistake a poppy for a red light, I'm guessing they probably shouldn't be at the controls of a train.' Another passenger commented that South West Trains should have foreseen the problem and placed the poppies further away from the tracks.

South West Trains confirmed that the poppies were taken down for 'health and safety reasons' and had been placed 'well away from the tracks' in the booking hall and ticket office.

MIND THE DOOR!

Although Brunel was a brilliant engineer, sometimes he made some quite elementary mistakes. At both Bristol and Bath stations he placed the train shed supports far too close to the edge of the platform, with the result that passengers emerging from their carriages were likely to crash into them.

Queen Victoria and King Louis Phillipe are descending at Gosport in October 1844. In the centre of the picture it can be seen that the clearance between the stone pillar and the coach is minimal.

Sir William Tite made an even greater blunder at Gosport. It was a superb structure and seemed a work of art, but its failure did not reveal itself until the first passenger trains worked into the station. The roof was supported by four very substantial stone pillars set at the four extremities and they came down flush with the platform edge. This had the result that when a train approached Gosport station and impatient passengers opened the doors before the train stopped, they found that they were wrenched out of their hands. The design was suitably modified with the original piers being cut back and cast iron supports and cross-members inserted away from the platform edge.

PENGUINS HATCH ON
||||||||||||||||||||||||||||||||||||||||||||||||||||||||||||||||||

EXETER ST DAVID'S STATION
||||||||||||||||||||||||||||||||||||||||||||||||||||||||||||||||||||||||||||

No, not the birds but the books. The story started in 1934 when Allen Lane, born 1902 and died 1970, was returning home after visiting his friend Agatha Christie at her home 'Greenway' near Dartmouth. Not having anything to read, he went to the station bookstall at St David's and was disappointed with the quality of the books on sale.

He realised there was a niche in the market for good-quality literature selling for the price of a packet of cigarettes – sixpence – a price everyone could afford. At a brainstorming meeting, his secretary Miss Cole suggested the title of the imprint be 'Penguin', this bird giving the idea of dignified flippancy.

Edward Young went to London Zoo and drew a penguin. Then a simple, yet effective, tri-band cover was designed with useful colour-coding, so you could see at a glance the type of book you required: green for thrillers, red for fiction, blue for biography etc.

Plaque at Exeter, St David's station.

These books could be sold for this low price because, as they were not new editions, publishers were quite willing to sell on royalties relatively inexpensively and the print runs on cheap paper were enormous. Profit margins were narrow and royalties limited.

Initially authors and booksellers were suspicious of this new imprint, but when Woolworth's and W.H. Smith & Sons stocked them in large quantities, sales took off. In the first month of trading, July 1935, 150,000 copies were sold in four days and a million in the first four months.

BEING NAMED AS LEAST-VISITED STATION

INCREASES PASSENGER TRAFFIC

The joint least-visited stations in Great Britain in 2018–19 were Denton in Greater Manchester and Stanlow & Thornton in Cheshire, each only having forty-six passengers. However, if previous holders of this status are anything to go by, these are likely to see a rise in numbers as there are always a number of people who are anxious to visit the least-visited stations.

Redcar British Steel station received only forty visitors in 2017–18, but 2019 saw 360 arrive on its platforms. Similarly Sugar Loaf, in rural Powys, was the quietest station in Wales 2016–17 with 228 passengers, but the following twelve months saw 1,824. Peter Joyce, a volunteer who helps look after the station, remarked: 'We've had people from the USA coming here because they've seen Sugar Loaf station referenced in books because it's so unused.'

AN UNDERGROUND STATION

NEVER OPENED

The deepest London Underground station is North End, between Hampsted and Golders Green. Set 221ft below the surface, it is the only closed underground station never to have been opened. No surface building was ever provided as the Heath is preserved and there would have been insufficient commuters to have made it economic.

A SHORT-LIVED STATION

One of the shortest-lived stations was Woodfield, Yorkshire, on the Meltham branch. It was only open for a month in 1874 and receipts averaged just over a shilling a day.

UNDERGROUND PASSENGERS PAY £100,000
A YEAR TO TRAVEL JUST ONE STOP

Tourists and others travelling on the London Underground spend £100,000 a year making the journey between two stations that are just a four-minute walk apart.

An average of 531 passengers travel between Covent Garden and Leicester Square stations in a typical week, with a further 331 making the journey in the opposite direction.

These are the network's two closest stations, their platforms less than 300yd apart and a train taking forty-five seconds to cover this distance. At £2.40 for a single ticket, it is an expensive alternative to a short stroll.

It is estimated that more than £100,000 is spent annually by passengers making a single journey between these stations. The true amount could be higher as these figures only cover customers using an Oyster, or contactless card.

Most people find it quicker, as well as cheaper, to walk the four minutes between Covent Garden and Leicester Square than to venture from street level down to the platform, wait for a train, make the journey, and then rise again to street level.

AN ASYLUM RAILWAY

Work on the construction of the East Sussex County Asylum (later known as Hellingly Hospital), north of Hailsham, Sussex, started in 1897. It not being easily accessible, in November 1899 the Asylum Committee agreed with the London, Brighton & South Coast Railway to build and maintain a mile-long branch line. Traffic would consist principally of coal and other materials conveyed in truckloads of not less than a ton. During the hospital's construction, traffic was worked by the contractor's locomotive, but in 1903 the line was electrified at 500v DC and operated by the East Sussex County Council. Power was supplied from the asylum's own generating station. The wire was suspended from poles set beside the track like a street tramway. For passengers, it is believed that this traffic began with the opening of the hospital on 20 July 1903. They travelled in a single-deck, four-wheeled tramcar seating twelve passengers purchased from Robert W. Blackwell & Company. At Hellingly a timber platform was constructed between the Eridge–Polegate line and the Asylum branch.

Freight traffic was handled by a 14hp steeple-cab electric locomotive capable of hauling two wagons up the ruling gradient of 1 in 50.

Passenger traffic ceased in 1931 and by 1954 only about one train ran daily. Although final closure was in March 1959, on 4 April 1959 the electric locomotive and a brake van borrowed from British Railways worked an enthusiasts' special.

Another hospital railway served Park Prewett Hospital near Basingstoke. The 1⅓-mile-long branch was worked by the London & South Western Railway. The line generally climbed to the terminus and had severe curves, some as tight as a seven-chain radius. As the First World War had started by the time the hospital was complete, from 1916 to 1921 it was used by invalids of the Canadian Army. It is possible that passenger trains may have run during its occupation by the Canadians, but there were none after 1924 until 1939 when a trial run of eight coaches was made with a locomotive at each end, proving to the authorities that curves and gradients made it unsuited to passenger trains.

Between the wars two goods trains usually ran weekly, one on Tuesday and the other on Friday. In order to avoid a breakaway on the steep gradients, trains were always propelled to the hospital.

London & North Western Railway 48ft fruit vans converted to ambulance cars at the Royal Victoria Hospital, Netley.

The hospital was required to maintain the track to the satisfaction of the railway company's engineer and in 1950, as he was dissatisfied, the Railway Executive gave notice that it was no longer prepared to work the line and would send coal and stores by road. The track was lifted by George Cohen in 1956.

The Royal Victoria Hospital, Netley, near Southampton, was built to accommodate military patients returning from overseas, initially from the Crimean War. It was a vast building, ¼ mile long. During its construction 2-2-0 locomotives were used, not to haul wagons, but to power mortar mixers.

In 1899 the War Department asked the London & South Western Railway to lay a branch just over ½ mile long to the hospital. Undulating, with gradients generally falling at 1 in 70 towards the hospital, it proved difficult to work, particularly in autumn when the rails were damp and covered with leaves.

The line opened on 18 April 1900. The platform was connected to the hospital by a covered way. The hospital's steam supply was used to warm the ambulance coaches stabled there. Between 24 August 1914 and 31 December 1918 approximately 1,200 hospital trains arrived at Netley. Immediately prior to the Second World War, rail movements on the line averaged about five annually. In 1942 a train arrived at Netley Hospital with about twenty horseboxes. Its occupants had been bombed out and brought to enjoy the grass in the hospital grounds. Very few hospital trains arrived at Netley until 1944, by which time it had been taken over by the American authorities. Following D-Day, casualties were brought by road, but moved by hospital trains to other hospitals for further treatment. In June and July 1944 approximately five fourteen- to sixteen-coach trains left the hospital daily. Greasy rails could cause a train to take forty-five minutes to reach the main line. The last train ran over the branch on 30 August 1955 and the hospital and station were demolished in 1967, though the chapel still survives.

AN UNUSUAL METHOD OF BRINGING

A TRAIN INTO A STATION

Waterloo was an 'open station' without fences or gates barring exit from the platforms. All Up passenger trains stopped at the ticket platform just outside the station. While the ticket collectors were at work, the locomotive was uncoupled from its train and a long rope substituted for the coupling. On restarting, once sufficient momentum had been achieved, this rope would be unhooked with the engine running 'light' into one road while some deft work by the pointsman diverted the slowly moving carriages into another. The practice, known as 'tailing in' or 'roping in', was also used at Windsor.

SCOTTISH ECONOMY

A curious example of a fare anomaly was in 1936 where Kincraig, a few miles south of Aviemore and 527¼ miles from Euston, had the normal third-class single fare of £3 5s 9d, but to all stations through Inverness to Invergordon, 599 miles from Euston, the same fare was charged. Legend has it that a certain Angus MacSandy, knowing this fact, demanded a ticket from Kincraig to Invergordon for nothing!

One thing was certain, he could not have legally travelled over that 71¾ miles of track without payment.

THE LABOURER DESERVES HIS REWARD

In the 1930s the standard charge for a third-class single ticket was 1½d a mile but there were exceptions. The London & North Western Railway had built the Runcorn Bridge across the Mersey, considerably shortening the journey from the Midlands and the South of England. Without special powers, the company would have been rewarded for its enterprise by receiving a lower fare due to the shortened journey, so Parliament sanctioned charging the fare as if the passenger had travelled via Warrington, making the fare for the 2½ miles between Runcorn and Ditton Junction 10d, rather than the 4½d one might expect.

LEFT ON THE PLATFORM

For a train on the Mid-Wales line there are over twenty stations to announce, and many are repeated because it needs to be explained that they are request stops only, requiring the guard to be notified. The entire announcement is read in both Welsh and English.

This takes so long that usually the train has left the station and is disappearing into the distance before the announcement ends.

THE SPIRITUAL RAILWAY

The death of two navvies killed on Christmas Eve 1845 while constructing the Ely–Peterborough line elicited this railway-inspired poetic epitaph inscribed on a tombstone at Ely Cathedral:

The line to Heaven by Christ was made
With heavenly truth the rails are laid
From Earth to Heaven the Line extends
To Life Eternal where it ends.

Repentance is the Station then
Where Passengers are taken in
No Fee for them is there to pay
For Jesus is himself the way.

God's Word is the first Engineer
It points the way to Heaven so clear,
Through tunnels dark and dreary here
It does the way to Glory steer.

God's Love the Fire, his Truth the Steam
Which drives the Engine and the Train
All you who would to Glory ride
Must come to Christ, in Him abide.

In First and Second, and Third Class,
Repentance, Faith and Holiness
You must the way to Glory gain
Or you with Christ will not remain.

Come then, poor Sinners, now's the time
At any Station on the Line
If you'll repent and turn from Sin
The train will stop and take you in.

THE DANGERS OF STEAM

In November 1910 Miss H.S. Fox of Halifax was crossing a footbridge at Low Town station, Pudsey, on the Great Northern Railway. The bridge was enveloped by steam from a locomotive standing below and a passenger hurrying in the opposite direction collided with her so violently that she was knocked unconscious and remained so for several days.

She brought a suit for damages against the GNR and was awarded a verdict, but the railway appealed and the Court of Appeal sent the case back for retrial.

The jury said that the GNR could not have foreseen that the accident would happen and so revoked the cost of damages.

A BIG BEER CELLAR

Only a fraction of Eurostar or domestic passengers using the undercroft of St Pancras station for shopping, or waiting in the departure lounge, are aware that it was originally a huge beer cellar. London's brewers produced a dark and cloudy ale and porter, whereas Burton's soft water made a clear and stable brew. When the development of railways meant it could be easily and cheaply transported to the capital, the Midland Railway erected a beer warehouse for Messrs Bass providing 6 acres of storage, or enough for 100,000 36-gallon barrels. So when St Pancras station was being planned in the 1870s, it was realised that its basement could provide vast, cool storage. Its architect, W.H. Barlow, cleverly designed it to accommodate as many barrels of Burton beer as possible, so the 720 supporting columns are carefully spaced at just over 14ft apart to achieve this end. Barrel storage at St Pancras began when the station opened in 1868 but finished in 1967.

How did the barrels get into the cellar? A central track between Platforms 4 and 5 ended in a wagon hoist that lowered them 20ft. These cellars were illuminated by gaslight.

Although the frontage block to the station, originally forming an hotel, is now an appreciated structure and Grade I listed, in its early days it had many critics, who believed Sir George Gilbert Scott's Gothic style to be extreme.

AN IMPORTANT LONDON TERMINUS

APPROACHED BY A SINGLE LINE

In the early twentieth century it was not generally known that an important London terminus was approached by a single line. At St Pancras, Up and Down trains passed over the same track, although this road was officially known as the Up line.

The Up road as far north of the station as the stop signal of the Cambridge Street signal box was used by all Up trains and also for empty Down trains running out of St Pancras, thus making it a single line.

COAL-SAVING TIP

In 1873 it was believed that the earth would shortly run out of coal. The London & South Western Railway discovered that if a coal fire was laid on a bed of chalk, it lasted much longer than when burning in an open grate at stations. LSWR passengers were fortunate to be able to still enjoy heat, but the Great Western had ordered all its waiting room and signal cabin fires to be extinguished.

TO WHICH STATION IS THE TRAIN GOING?

The original station at Godalming was a terminus, but in 1859 the town was placed on a through line and given a new station. The problem for horse cab drivers was that a terminating train could use either station and the decision as to which station was used was made by the signalman at Godalming Junction.

This meant that the cab drivers developed the ploy of gathering at the Charterhouse Arms and listening for the locomotive's whistle, which would tell them whether they should gallop off to the old station or to the new. Apparently not all the signalman's decisions were sensible, as on at least one occasion a train scheduled to go beyond Godalming was sent to the old station and had to be reversed out before it could resume its journey. The old station closed on 1 May 1897, after which there were no more problems.

FIRST WORLD WAR AIR RAID

A South Eastern & Chatham Railway guard described a German air raid on London on 7 July 1917:

> We had just started our journey when I heard the noise of anti-aircraft guns. Looking out of my van, I saw a large number of aeroplanes, but for a little while I could not tell whether they were British or German. Then to my consternation several of the machines descended in the direction of my train. The next moment there was a terrific bang, followed by deafening explosions. I managed to keep pretty cool, though the experience was most nerve-shattering. Peeping out again, I caught sight of an aeroplane flying very low and apparently heading so as to get right over our engine. Like a flash a second machine dived towards him, and this proved to be a British aeroplane. The two airmen fought each other, and so near were they to the train that I could hear the rattle of the machine

guns. By now the engine-driver had put on speed. Once again I looked out, just in time to see the combatants climbing rapidly one after the other. After a while they were lost to view, and from the way they were flying I should say the German was being chased towards the sea.

A POOR WELCOME GIVEN
AT EARLY GWR STATIONS

In its early days the Great Western Railway excluded from platforms those not travelling by train, which meant that friends of the passengers were unable to see them off. To counter this criticism, the GWR provided platform passes for those wishing to see off or meet friends at stations, but these were difficult to procure.

To obtain a pass it was necessary to be at a station for a considerable length of time before the train was due to arrive or start, as the booking clerk had to write on the pass the name and address of the applicant, stamp it and then send it to the station superintendent for signature before it could be used.

Passengers who were travelling were not allowed on a platform until their train was approaching, but confined to waiting rooms – a most apposite title under the circumstances.

A HIGHLY DANGEROUS PRACTICE

In 1917 a North Eastern Railway guard was killed at Eaglescliffe through being compelled to ride on the front buffer of a train that was being propelled, instead of being hauled. He fell off the wagon and the train passed over him. NER men were naturally alarmed at the number of trains being worked in this dangerous manner over various sections of the line.

AN INTERNATIONAL RAIL TERMINAL
BUILT ON A RUBBISH HEAP

On the site of St Pancras station was the spot known with the cockney's humorous irony as 'Belle Isle', where the dustbins of the whole of London had been emptied. Mountains of unsavoury refuse were surrounded by wretched hovels. Readers of Dickens will recall the Golden Dustman in *Our Mutual Friend:* his dust heaps were at Battle Bridge, close by.

SWEEPS SENT TO SIT NEXT TO GENTLEMEN

In 1841 the third-class passenger was despised by the railway companies and travellers were encouraged to purchase first- or second-class tickets. Perhaps the most obnoxious statement regarding them was made by the chairman of the Northern & Eastern Railway: 'No railway establishment could be considered complete without two or three sweeps with their soot bags. Whenever I saw an individual respectfully dressed getting into a third-class carriage, I would send a sweep along to sit with him.'

WASTED FOOD

Despite the food shortage in the First World War, it could sometimes be wasted through slow transport. On 20 June 1917, 1,000 bales of bacon were condemned at the Great Eastern Railway depot, Minories, after being held there for five weeks – it was poor quality and eventually sold for manure. The following day, 800 bales stored for four weeks were going rotten and were eventually sold to soap manufacturers.

MR VERSUS LNWR ORTHOGRAPHY

Bradshaw's Railway Guide stated in a footnote that from Boxmoor to Hemel Hempstead (London & North Western) it was over 1½ miles to Hemel Hempsted (Midland). The Midland time table also omitted the 'a', but the Railway Clearing House used an 'a'. Obviously Bradshaw desired to serve two masters in the spelling of Hempstead.

RAILWAY PRISON CELL

In the courtyard of Euston station was a small, one-storey stone building near the Drummond Street gate. People arrested by London & North Western Railway policemen were taken there and questioned before being handed to the Metropolitan Police.

HOW THE METROPOLITAN & DISTRICT RAILWAY SPEEDED TRAIN BOARDING

In 1919 a passenger-hustler made an appearance at the District's Victoria station during rush hours. The *modus operandi* of the hustler, officially called a controller, was that when a train had been standing at a platform for thirty seconds, as timed by his stopwatch, he blew a siren, which continued to blare until the train left. This noise encouraged passengers to board faster. The same plan was utilised at Charing Cross and Tottenham Court Road stations.

WHAT WAS A RAILWAY STATION WORTH?

In 1920 when the redundant station connected with the Georgetown Shell Filling Factory near Paisley was auctioned, the following figures were realised: north platform £1,000; south platform £540; two platform shelters £382; covered footbridge £100; three railway sidings, respectively £680, £570 and £520, the rate being just over £2 per yard.

2

TRAVELLING BY TRAIN

THE DANGER OF STRING BAGS
IN RAILWAY TRAINS

You may not think it, but string shopping bags can be dangerous in a railway carriage.

One lady recalls that in the 1950s, while travelling in a crowded train, her aunt's bag became entangled with a gentleman's trouser buttons. This fact remained unobserved until she stood up and tried to leave the compartment and found the man extremely embarrassed. Although the zip fastener has solved this particular problem, today there are navel piercings to worry about.

HOW THIRD-CLASS PASSENGERS
COULD TRAVEL IN FIRST CLASS

Many of the Great Western Railway's slip coaches were of semi-corridor design, generally having a guard's compartment at each end with two first- and five third-class compartments between. Side corridors gave access to lavatories, but not to the guard's compartment. This enabled deceitful third-class passengers, when

Bath Spa station on 9 September 1933. In the centre, two slip-coaches have been detached from the non-stop train on the right. A steam railmotor has just left the station on the other track.

the train had left Paddington on its non-stop run to Bath, to give another meaning to the term 'slip coach' when they slipped into a first-class compartment.

A GWR SEASON TICKET ALMOST 2FT LONG

Most season tickets are just for one length of track between two named stations. Although this is fine for most people, traders need a more extensive coverage, so for them the Great Western Railway issued Trader's Tickets.

No. 705 issued in the mid 1930s cost £135 15*s* and was almost 2ft long. Fortunately, it was designed to be folded concertina-wise into an area no larger than a normal season ticket and was placed in a protective wallet

Great Western Railway ticket No. 705 valid from 21 March 1934 until 20 March 1935 is nearly 2ft in length; it could be folded and placed in a wallet.

AN ECCENTRIC DUKE

The 5th Duke of Portland's estate was at Welbeck Abbey and the Duke himself had an eccentric mode of travel.

His estate had lengthy road tunnels. Exiting from his home, he entered his carriage with the blinds down and was driven for over a mile through a tunnel to Worksop Road & Worksop station, where his carriage was loaded on a flat wagon and coupled to a London train. At King's Cross it was unloaded and he was driven to his London home in Cavendish Square, still with the blinds down.

A RESOURCEFUL PORTER

In the 1930s a boy leaned out of the carriage window to wish his mother goodbye. She asked: 'Now you've got your ticket safe, haven't you?' As he showed it to her, he dropped it between the platform and the train. She then summoned a porter, who pondered over the situation.

He took down the long Cornish Riviera roof board, collected a cake of soap from the coach toilet, dabbed it on the end of the board and picked up the ticket by prodding it with the soapy end, which caused it to adhere.

SAILING ALONG A RAILWAY LINE

Wind power was used for propulsion from the very early days of railways – not for ecological reasons, but because it happened to be practical.

The first example was probably at Neath in 1698, while a later example was from Patrington to Spurn Head and used by lifeboatmen, lighthouse keepers and visiting civilians.

It originated in the First World War as the Spurn Military Railway to give access to Green Battery, Spurn Head and Godwin Battery, Kilnsea. In post-war years the line was abandoned, but in October 1922 two local men brought it back into use. They found a four-wheeled trolley and fixed a gaff-rigged sail that in a previous life had been a cinema screen in the garrison YMCA hut.

The fastest time for the 3 miles from Spurn to Kilnsea was three minutes, giving an average speed of 60mph – rather in excess of that obtained on most light railways. It could run in all winds except a dead north wind, or a calm, and there were very few calm days at Spurn Head. (Personally, I am suspicious of the speed of 60mph. Probably a stopwatch was not used and with an ordinary watch a reading could be inaccurate, perhaps half a minute out at the start and half a minute at the end, giving a time of four minutes, or a much more reasonable speed of 45mph.)

Similarly, on the Thames below Gravesend there was a narrow-gauge steam railway serving works at Cliffe, with the unusual gauge of 3ft 8½in. The works closed about 1920, but the line continued to be used informally. In the 1930s the lighthouse keeper, J.W. Slater, used to sail for 2 or 3 miles down the line each day having 'equipped the chassis of a truck, originally belonging to the cement company that owned the quarry, with two masts carrying lug sails and a jib, and thus makes full use of the stiff sea breezes that blow across the exposed lonely lower stretches of the Thames.' When the wind failed to blow, the alternative motive power was Mr Slater's donkey.

BALANCED INCLINES

Steam locomotives were not very good at climbing hills, so engineers planning a line tried to keep it as level as possible. Sometimes the terrain made this impossible, but if the load descending an incline was greater than that going up, a balanced incline held the answer.

Runaways were not unknown on inclined planes. Here, Midland Railway wagons have ended in a catch pit on the Cromford & High Peak line.

You simply constructed a double track with a large wheel set horizontally at the top and linked a cable from the loaded train at the top, to an empty (or lightly loaded) train at the bottom. As the heavy train descended, it hauled up the lighter one. A cheaper alternative to a complete double track was a single track top and bottom, with a passing loop in the centre.

This system was useful when collieries were set above a railway. It had the disadvantage that there was usually at least one occasion when the cable would snap and a train come hurtling down the incline.

EQUALITY OF THE SEXES?

In 1848 the Manchester & Leeds Railway issued day tickets to Blackpool for 1s 6d gentlemen and 1s 0d ladies. This concession was withdrawn when it was discovered that men were masquerading as females to get cheaper tickets.

The following year the men were even worse off. A handbill of 1849 publicised an excursion from Maudland to Fleetwood on 6 August and women and children were offered tickets at half the price of those charged to men. It suggested that 'employers who do not arrange trips on their own account, may avail themselves of this opportunity of sending down any of the sick or other hands whom they may be desirous of treating. A steamer will ply through the day to take persons round the Light-house at 2d each.'

The excursionists had a particularly exciting ride, as for almost 2 miles on the approach to Fleetwood, the line ran partly along a stone-faced embankment and partly on wooden piles. Problems with this approach led to its abandonment when an alternative route was made the following year.

PIGEON SPECIALS

Well into the 1960s, pigeon specials at weekends were an important sideline to the railway's parcels business. On Friday night/Saturday morning racing pigeon specials ran to various parts of the country.

For example, between 8.00 p.m. and 8.30 p.m. on Fridays, pigeon clubs set up tables at Bath, fanciers counting the birds and loading the baskets on long barrow. These were then placed in vans and taken to Mangotsfield and made up into a train with similar vans from Bristol bound for the north.

Porters disliked handling pigeon baskets because of the smell and mess of their occupants. Incoming pigeons were released from Bath Goods Yard, which was open with no overhead wires.

Some trains shipped pigeons to Weymouth or Southampton for a sea voyage to northern France, where they would be released.

AN UNUSUAL WAY OF DETERMINING FARES

In the early 1840s, the Manchester & Birmingham Railway fares were determined on the space required by passengers. If there were four passengers in a compartment between Manchester and London the fare was £2 16s 0d each, but if they were allowed to squeeze in a further two passengers, the fare was only £2 12s 0d.

RACE BETWEEN TRAIN AND PLANE

On 15 June 1928 a contest on which form of transport could reach Scotland first was arranged between a train and a plane. Although not strictly a race, the simultaneous flight and non-stop journey between London and Edinburgh was seen as a means of direct comparison between the two modes of transport, and made in the full glare of publicity.

So that this particular train could be identified from the air, one of the carriages had 'Flying Scotsman' painted on the roof.

The day began with breakfast for about fifty passengers at the Savoy Hotel, London. The entire airborne party of twenty-one was present, together with a small fraction of the 300 train passengers who had booked seats in advance.

Both aircraft and train passengers left the Savoy Hotel together. Although the plane, an Armstrong Whitworth Argosy biplane *City of Glasgow* with a maximum speed of 115mph was faster, it had to stop twice to refuel.

When the Flying Scotsman reached Edinburgh Waverley station eleven minutes early it was declared the winner, the air passengers coming from Edinburgh's Turnhouse airport having been delayed by traffic and not appearing until four minutes after the train's arrival.

IS A CHILD'S PEDAL CAR A VELOCIPEDE?

In 1910 the Great Western Railway contended that a child's pedal-driven motor car was really a velocipede and therefore chargeable as such. However, a judge at West London County Court decided it was a toy and therefore should be conveyed at the usual rates for goods under that description.

A RIVAL TO HOLMES

Railways have always experienced problems with fare dodgers. About 1920, after an Up train had just left Woking, a gentleman with a bland smile tried to pass the ticket barrier; no, he had not come by train, he was just seeing a friend off.

The foreman ticket collector was dubious and – having, with a Sherlock Holmes-esque scrutiny, observed certain incriminating facts – suggested that he must have come by train. Met by an indignant denial, he replied, 'Then how is it that the soles of your boots are dry?'

It had been raining all morning in Woking.

A GIGANTIC TRAIN

When Queen Victoria was to pass through Linlithgow in 1842, 4,000 people availed themselves of the opportunity presented by the Slamannan Railway to see her. One train carried no fewer than 1,500 passengers in 110 vehicles, with four engines at the front and one in the rear. At least some of the vehicles were very small coal wagons as they only accommodated about fourteen passengers.

AN EARLY USE OF RADIO

The Stratford-upon-Avon & Midland Junction Railway, although a small company, was at the forefront of technology. By 1910 all its coaches were electrically lit – more than could be said for the larger railway companies. Then, in July 1912, a radio message was transmitted from a train betweens Ettington and Stratford, it being reported:

> Representatives of railway companies, universities and scientific bodies are today inspecting the Von Kramer wireless inductive railophone system for signalling to and from trains to stations. With this system it is possible to stop trains in motion by pressing a button in a signal box. This telegram was dispatched wirelessly from a moving train by the inventor.

MULLER'S LIGHTS

In July 1864 Thomas Briggs, a 69-year-old banking clerk, caught the 9.50 p.m. Broad Street–Poplar service on the North London Railway. A German immigrant, Franz Muller, in the same first-class compartment, beat him viciously, stole his gold watch and chain and gold-rimmed glasses, and threw him out on to the railway line. At the next station, a passenger entering the compartment, found blood on the floor and raised the alarm.

Soon afterwards, Mr Briggs was spotted by an engine driver and taken to the Mitford, a public house in Cadogan Terrace, Bow, for treatment before being taken home, where he died the next morning.

Police Inspector Tanner eventually discovered that Franz Muller had left for New York. The inspector boarded a faster vessel, arrived first and arrested the German, who was taken back to England and, after trial at the Old Bailey, hanged in November 1864. That trial was sensation for two reasons: it was the first

An 1868 cartoon in *Punch* illustrates the disadvantages of a Muller's light.

murder on a British train and Muller had reached New York before he was captured.

In addition to stealing his watch and glasses, the murderer stole the victim's tall top hat, which he had cut down into a shorter style, either to elude recognition or for convenience when he was escaping. The 'Muller cut-down' as it was known, became a fashion trend.

In an effort to prevent a repetition of this incident, spy holes were made between compartments – these nosey-parker windows being dubbed 'Muller's Lights'.

CARRYING PRISONERS

Until the advent of motor transport, railways were used for conveying prisoners and warders, usually travelling in a reserved compartment. A requirement that prisoners should wear a broad arrow when travelling was abolished in 1921.

It is believed that the London & South Western Railway carried more prisoners than any other line, and on almost any weekday, convicts in the charge of prison warders could be seen at Waterloo. Prisoners to Dartmoor travelled to Tavistock by the 9.00 a.m., 11.00 a.m. and 1.00 p.m. trains, while those to Portland used the 9.20 a.m. or 12.30 p.m. Weymouth expresses and those to Parkhurst patronised the 9.00 a.m. or 12.10 p.m.

During the First World War, because sometimes as many as thirty-five naval prisoners could be carried on a Highland Railway train, for extra security some compartments in carriages were converted into semi-permanent cells to hold prisoners from Invergordon or Scapa Flow.

During the Second World War, German prisoners-of-war were carried by train and in order to deter escapes, signalmen were asked to try and avoid offering such a train an adverse signal.

RACE BETWEEN A PIGEON
AND AN EXPRESS TRAIN

In 1930 the *Kent Messenger* organised a London–Dover race between a pigeon and the Golden Arrow express train. The pigeon, a Waterine No. R. P. 278 1360, was released by Kousin Mac, the newspaper's children's correspondent, and witnessed by a top-hatted station master. The Golden Arrow was headed by a Lord Nelson-class 4-6-0.

Both the train and pigeon left Victoria six-and-half seconds before 11.00 am. The pigeon clocked in at Dover at 12.37 p.m., while the train arrived at Dover Marine at 12.35 p.m., two minutes earlier.

The *Kent Messenger* held a competition offering a guinea prize for the person whose estimate was nearest to the pigeon's time. A Staplehurst reader guessed one hour thirty-seven minutes and ten seconds – only a few seconds out.

PROBLEMS EARLY TRAVELLERS FACED

WHEN PURCHASING A RAILWAY TICKET

When the Liverpool & Manchester Railway opened in 1830, intending passengers were required to apply twenty-four hours in advance, giving their name, address, place of birth, age, occupation and the reason for their journey. This enabled the station agent, as early station masters were termed, to satisfy himself that 'the applicant desires to travel for a just and lawful cause'.

At that time, many regarded rail travel as a danger to the stability of society, which would, in the words of the Duke of Wellington, 'act as a premium to the lower orders to go uselessly wandering about the country'.

THRIFTY FOOTBALL FAN'S FIFTY-SIX

RAIL TICKETS TO ONE GAME

In January 2017 Jonny Heywood wanted to take a trip with his girlfriend to watch Newcastle play Oxford United in the FA Cup. Wishing to obtain the cheapest fare, he used a split ticket website and saved £30. The journey took four hours and nine minutes, and they stayed on the same train.

Mr Heywood told the *Daily Telegraph*:

> There were 56 tickets, so 28 each for me and my girlfriend and we split them into four envelopes so it was manageable. The only hassle was our reservation changed every couple of stops so we sat in two unreserved seats for the whole journey.
>
> Sadly the journey was a waste of time because my girlfriend ended up slipping over as she entered the ground, burst her lip open, went unconscious and sat in hospital for four hours.

If you're interested, his team lost 3-0.

EXPENSIVE TICKETS

The *Daily Telegraph* of 2 February 2017 revealed that an open return from Wick in the north of Scotland to Penzance in Cornwall – Britain's longest railway journey – was priced at £467.40 on Trainline. From Shanklin on the Isle of Wight to Buxton in Derbyshire was said to be the UK's most expensive rail journey, an anytime return costing £501.40.

UNFAIR FARE

In 2017 a commuter from Blackpool who normally made the 228-mile trip from Preston to London, found he could cut £260, or almost 75 per cent, off the cost of his return ticket by boarding the train at Lancaster, 25 miles further from the capital.

Then, on his journey by Virgin train to Euston, he was accused by the guard of getting on at Preston and told he should pay the £356 required to travel from there.

When he refused this charge, police were on the platform waiting for him, questioning him for thirty minutes and causing him to miss a business meeting. Virgin officials checked CCTV cameras and established that he had, indeed, got on at Lancaster and held a valid ticket. In recompense he was only offered 50 per cent off his next trip.

Other contemporary confusing rail fare costs were: Leeds–Edinburgh £205 return, but if you travelled 22 miles to York you could get a return to Edinburgh for £63.40; Sandwell & Dudley–Euston was £176, but if you went 8 miles to Birmingham New Street a return was only £54; a Stockport–Plymouth return cost £273.80, but if single tickets were booked each way the cost fell to £110.20.

A TURTLE & ORCHID TRAIN

Once a fortnight – usually every alternate Thursday – a turtle and orchid train steamed into Waterloo station a few minutes after 10.00 a.m. The 100–150 turtles came from the West Indies and seeing long rows of them lying on their backs was an extraordinary sight. The orchids, packed in cases, came principally from the West Indies or Brazil.

YOU LEARN BY EXPERIENCE

The London & South Western's main line to Exeter opened on 18 July 1860. Within a fortnight of this event, a gentleman and three ladies journeyed to Axminster by the last Up train, *Pulman's Weekly News & Advertiser* recording:

Many others had the same idea, and they disembarked at their destination. However, the gentleman and ladies sat still until, as they imagined, the crowd on the platform would disperse and their path made easier. Alas their behaviour 'was not in accord with the practice followed by ordinary railway travellers and not understood by railway officials'. Ample time was given for all to alight whilst 'Axminster! Axminster!' was loudly proclaimed by the numerous staff. Subsequently, the signal was given for the

Horse-drawn vehicles wait at Axminster station *c.* 1905 for passengers such as the gentleman and three ladies.

train to start and away it went. At this point a carriage window was opened and a shout of 'Stop! Stop! – four of us to get out' was issued.

It was all too late. The shouts only reached the bystanders on the platform for the engine driver was too far ahead and out of earshot. The result was that the onlookers only laughed aloud. The gentleman kept shouting, even waving his hat, as the train passed over the level crossing. All was to no avail. The driver could not see or hear him as he was looking ahead, not at the train behind. Consequently our party were 'whirled on to the next station', from where they had to hire a carriage so that they could return to their intended destination. No doubt they would all master train travel in the future, but a necessary lesson had been taught.

MISSING PASSENGER!

The *Dundee Advertiser* for 17 December 1872 reported: 'On the arrival of a train at a northern station a few days ago it was discovered that one of the passengers was missing. The missing one, a pig weighing 35 stones, was found grazing in a field beside the railway. It had leapt from a truck while the train was at full speed but was not injured.'

The Cornishman of 3 August 1882 reported that a dog being taken to a dog show at Stockton-on-Tees nibbled a hole in its basket and leapt out of the guard's van window. When the owner reached the show he found the dog, a Bedlington terrier, waiting for him on the bench. He had been found loose on the railway, but his destination label enabled him to be sent on the next train. He won third prize in the show.

FIGHT TO SECURE READING

TO LONDON PASSENGERS

In the mid-nineteenth century, the Great Western Railway only ran one third-class train daily between Reading and London, so most travellers had to travel second class at a return fare of 6s 8d. The South Eastern Railway provided a fast train from Reading to London Bridge at a return fare for only 4s 6d second class. London Bridge was much nearer the City, and to reach it from Paddington required a bus ride, so the longer 66-mile SER route was almost as quick, more convenient and much cheaper than the GWR's 36-mile journey, and most people used the SER service.

However, this was not the end of the story. The London & South Western Railway had running powers into the SER Reading station, so it reduced its return fare to 4s 6d for a second-class return to Waterloo and, this being only a journey of 44 miles, passengers transferred their patronage from the SER to the LSWR. In retaliation, the SER reduced its fare and the LSWR followed suit; then reduction followed reduction until both lines carried passengers from Reading to London for 1s 6d single or 2s 0d return, which was only a penny for every 5 miles using the SER.

A STRIKING STORY

Some Bristol businessmen, rather than living in the smoky and noisy city, preferred the sea breezes of Portishead, travelling the 9 miles or so by train.

On 18 August 1911, a large number of such businesspeople living in Portishead and working in Bristol, anticipating that the General Strike would disorganise the train services, arrived to catch the first train, the 6.55 a.m. They were met by the station master and told what boiled down to 'Tough luck, it's cancelled', though, this being 1911, he expressed it more deferentially.

One of these horse-drawn vehicles outside Portishead station *c.* 1905 may well have been the one hired by the businessmen.

Two gentlemen, anxious to reach Bristol, hired the only taxicab of which the town could boast. The other passengers used their initiative and hired a brake and pair from the local livery stable.

The two in the taxi felt less superior when, after proceeding only a few hundred yards, it emitted an ominous noise and as the driver turned his head to ascertain the cause, the taxi mounted the pavement and nearly overturned. It stopped and an inspection revealed that the driving chain had snapped.

While the driver was attempting to make a repair, a private motorist came along and offered them a lift. This they gladly accepted and on their way to Bristol met the horse brake returning. The motorists were also beaten into Bristol by a further group from Portishead, which had used bicycles. Some of the commuters wisely decided to stay overnight in Bristol to avoid problems the next morning.

PARCEL FORCE

It is hard to believe today that tube trains once dealt with parcels. In 1911 the Central London Railway decided to collect as well as deliver parcels. Tricycle carriers branded 'Central London Railway (Tube). Lightning Parcels Express' carried out deliveries at each end of the line, and the system was so efficient that packages could be conveyed from the City to the West End in well under forty minutes.

The service was expanded to enable people to book parcels to any station on the Great Western or Great Central Railway and in 1913 made a profit of £702 17s 1d.

Central London Railway electric locomotive No. 19 stands at Shepherd's Bush depot in March 1900.

FREE TRAVEL

In August 1831 one Liverpool newspaper proprietor asked to be allowed to send parcels of papers by early train to Manchester free of charge. Rather surprisingly, the company agreed on condition that the parcels were called for on arrival and that the railway was not held responsible for their safety.

DISLIKE CHANGING TRAINS? NO PROBLEM
– HIRE A SPECIAL

In 1905, Harry Payne Whitney arrived at Liverpool from the USA and wished to take friends to a shooting box near Middleton-in-Teesdale. Rather than go through the bother of changing trains en route, he ordered a special for £80.

WHY THE GUARD LEFT THE DOG
AT TEMPLECOMBE

The rule that dogs were not allowed to be taken into a compartment was strictly enforced on the London & South Western Railway.

A young lady en route to Exeter entered a carriage at Waterloo with a fine specimen of a Pekinese dog. The vigilant guard called the lady's attention to the breach of regulations. She replied that the dog was 'such a dear and would hurt no one', but the guard insisted on compliance with the order and offered to take the dog to his van.

The lady refused to let him touch the dog and took the animal to the guard's van herself, where she fastened him to a box. Giving the dog a final caress, she gave the guard the emphatic instruction 'not to touch the dog' before returning to her seat.

Arriving at Exeter, Queen Street, she appeared at the luggage van to claim her pet. After searching for, and failing to find him, she enquired of the guard: 'Where is my dog?' 'At Templecombe, madam,' he replied. 'You strictly charged me not to touch him, and as you had fastened him to a box that was labelled to Templecombe, I put the box out there and your dog, of necessity, followed.'

PASSENGERS SHOULD NOT LEAN OUT

OF THE WINDOW

Boys' books on railways used to feature a page or two telling of the Travelling Post Office, whereby mail could be picked up, or dropped, while the train was moving at 60mph or more – exciting stuff.

The operation was not entirely risk free. Pouches from trains sometimes bounded over hedges, or under carriage wheels. In February 1889 a young lady was travelling on the night mail, which left Aberdeen at 1.00 a.m. and was to arrive at Euston 3.50 p.m. Approaching Beattock station, north of Carlisle about 8.00 a.m., she unwisely thrust her head out of the carriage window and struck the suspended leather satchel containing the mail, knocking it off its support standard.

Stunned by the blow, she remained in the leaning-out-of-the-window position. The next pouch to be collected was 14 miles ahead at Lockerbie. This pouch was received into the net correctly, but 5¾ miles further on at Ecclefechen, her head struck another pouch and released it from the standard.

There were two ladies in the compartment with her, presumably asleep as they were unaware of what had occurred until the train reached Ecclefechen. Here their screams attracted the

Fortunately no one is looking out of a carriage window as this London & North Western Railway express is about to collect a mail bag from the pillar.

attention of a passenger in the next compartment, who pulled the communication cord and stopped the train. The unfortunate lady was found unconscious and died of concussion a few hours later.

The Board of Trade held the necessary inquiry. It found that the existence of a heavy obstruction weighing, if full, about ¾ hundredweight and hanging from 8 to 13in (and closer if the train or bag was oscillating) from the side of a carriage, just about the level of the head of a passenger leaning out of a carriage window, was certainly most dangerous.

It was surprising that no accident had occurred before. To alleviate the problem was difficult. The collecting net could not project further, nor the pouch suspended at a height above the carriage windows, as to do either would have involved a net too high to pass under the many over bridges; while if the pouch were placed below the window sill level it would interfere with the delivery apparatus.

The solution was for the Board of Trade to instruct that the Post Office vehicles were to be placed at the front of the train, so that a pouch would be collected before a passenger coach reached a support standard.

MANY PASSENGERS AND LOW FARES, OR HIGH FARES AND FEW PASSENGERS

The Canterbury & Whitstable Railway was cited as an example of large traffic due to low fares. Between February and November 1840, when the fare was $9d$, receipts were only £9,388. On 1 February 1841, the fare was reduced to $6d$ and in the following ten months fares amounted to £23,719 – an increase of 155 per cent, while the number of passengers increased by about 400 per cent.

BRITISH RAILWAYS IN THE FIRST WORLD WAR

The outbreak of war on 4/5 August 1914 had serious implications for the London & South Western Railway on account of the great uses made of its Southampton Docks and the fact that the company served Aldershot and Bulford camps. In fact, a total of 176 army camps were served by the LSWR.

When war was declared, the War Office gave the Railway Executive Committee sixty hours to assemble locomotives and rolling stock to convey the British Expeditionary Force to Southampton. This was achieved in just forty-eight hours and embarkation began on 9 August and was completed by 31 August, during which time 5,006 officers, 125,171 men, 38,805 horses, 344 guns, 1,575 other vehicles, 277 motor vehicles, 1,802 motor cycles and 6,406 tons of stores had been shipped from Southampton using 711 trains. The busiest day was 22 August, when seventy-three trains were dealt with, eight timed to arrive between 6.12 a.m. and 7.36 a.m., another eight between 12.12 p.m. and 1.36 p.m. and twenty-one between 2.12 p.m. and 6.12 p.m. This rapid arrival of the British Expeditionary Force surprised the Germans.

Apart from carrying troops and their supplies and the wounded to hospital, railways were affected by the war in other ways. Due to the danger of mines in the North Sea, some coastal traffic was diverted to rail. From 5 November 1914, the blinds of carriages in the London district had to be drawn after dark so an air raid notice was displayed in every compartment. The wording used by the companies varied, one example being:

Great Northern Railway Lighting Regulations – London Area
It is necessary at present for the blinds to be kept down in a lighted train in the London area, and passengers are requested to assist by carrying out this regulation.
London (King's Cross Station)
November 1914
By Order

Windows in Midland Railway guards' vans that had no blinds had brown pigment smeared over to render them opaque. As North London Railway coaches were not provided with blinds, the drop lights were painted over with a red pigment.

The inhabitants of the Isle of Sheppey (on which was sited Sheerness Dockyard and Naval Air Station) were not allowed to leave the island, nor visitors allowed to enter without a pass, unless they travelled by the South Eastern & Chatham Railway. The Chief Constable issued the order: 'Residents of Sheerness wishing to proceed to places outside the Isle of Sheppey must do so by train and not by road.'

To ensure proper feeding of soldiers travelling by rail, the War Office promised:

> Arrangements have been made with all the railway companies in Great Britain on whose systems there are refreshment rooms for certain standard meals to be provided, if required by individual soldiers or small parties, on payment of 1s cash.
>
> A soldier to receive: Dinner (11 am–3 pm) (a) 2 meat sandwiches, ham or beef, total weight about 2 oz; (b) buttered roll and 2 oz Cheddar cheese; (c) meat pie about 6 oz; (d) 1 pint tea or coffee or large mineral water.
>
> Breakfast (5 am–11 am) and tea (3 pm–10 pm) The same as dinner under (a) and (d) plus 4 slices of bread and butter, or roll and butter, and 2 hard-boiled eggs or one sausage.

From 15 November 1914 all departures for France and Flushing were only from Victoria station and passengers and luggage searched to guard against secret information being taken across the Channel – searching, of course, was a novel concept in 1914, not a familiar feature like today. After booking, passengers were placed in separate rooms for men and women and male and female staff under the orders of Scotland Yard detectives searched them. Following the search, passengers were conducted to the train and under no circumstances allowed to communicate with anyone.

At the commencement of hostilities, railways patriotically renamed locomotives that had carried Austrian and German names. Great Western No. 4017 *Knight of the Black Eagle* became *Knight of Liege*, and London & North Western No. 372 *Germanic* had a thick red line drawn through the Hunite adjective and carried new name plates above bearing the honourable name of *Belgic*. LNWR No. 2583 *Teutonic* was re-christened *The Tsar*.

SPEEDING FISH

In 1913 the fastest goods train in Great Britain was run by the Great Northern Railway. It was the 2.26 a.m. York–King's Cross for fish and perishables. It took four hours nine minutes to cover the 188 miles at an average speed of 47mph. The GNR also ran the second fastest train at 44mph. The London & North Western's fastest goods ran at 43mph from Carlisle to London with fish and perishables. At the other end of the speed table, the slowest goods, as opposed to minerals, were run by the South Eastern & Chatham, the London, Brighton & South Coast and the Midland railways all at an average of 4mph.

VEGETABLES TRAVEL CHEAPLY BY TRAIN

In 1914 the cost of transporting food by train was so insignificant, it was almost negligible. Transport for the 88 miles from Evesham to Nottingham was a penny for 9lb; the same for 21lb of potatoes for the 72 miles from Wisbech to Nottingham. Transporting strawberries from Swanwick to London cost 3 farthings for 4lb, or a penny per lb if you were to send them to Glasgow (475 miles) instead. It cost one penny for every 4lb of cherries transported the 227 miles from Sittingbourne to Manchester, while meat went from Birkenhead to London at the rate of 7lb for a penny and fish the 221 miles from Grimsby to London at a penny for 6lb.

MAKING PLATFORMS SUITABLE FOR SKIRTS

In 1914 Blakeney Rural District Council in the Forest of Dean asked the Great Western Railway to consider raising the height of the local railway platform as it had been found that ladies wearing fashionable tight skirts were unable to reach the steps of a carriage.

No ladies with tight skirts appear in this photograph of Awre for Blakeney station.

CHEAP WORKMEN'S FARES

As the Cheap Trains Act of 1883 did not specifically define who was entitled to a cheap workman's fare, anyone who presented himself within the hours workmen's trains were run, that is up to 8.00 a.m., was allowed to travel at a reduced fare.

In 1920, as workmen were considered to earn high wages, it did not seem fair that they should be able to travel at a cheaper rate, and Lord Ashfield, on behalf of the underground railway companies, said:

I think that workmen's fares should be abolished entirely so far as the Underground railways are concerned. The fares which prevail throughout the whole of the day should, I think, apply to all classes. I say that for two reasons. First I do not think that one section of the community should be allowed to travel cheaply at the expense of another, and secondly the change in social conditions makes the question of workmen's fares almost inoperative. There are far more genuine bona-fide working people carried after the time the workmen's tickets cease to be issued, with the result that the great mass of the working people who can no better afford to pay the ordinary fare than can those who travel at the earlier hours, are really making up the loss incurred by the issue of workmen's tickets.

A RAILWAY COMPANY GIVES PASSENGERS

THE COLD SHOULDER

The only Sunday train on the Tidworth branch of the Great Western Railway ran from Ludgershall to Tidworth for the benefit of servicemen returning from leave. In the interests of economy, instead of going to the expense of providing a branch train between Ludgershall and Tidworth, this Sunday service was worked by the front portion of the Andover to Swindon train. This meant that the rear half of the train was left standing at Ludgershall until the engine returned from Tidworth to take it forward. No engine for thirty minutes meant no heating, and in winter vociferous complaints were often made that the Swindon portion grew very cold while waiting engineless.

PARTY TIME

On 10 April 1963 a four-coach restaurant car special hauled by 45XX class 2-6-2T No. 4555 left Brent at 18.55 for Kingsbridge. By the time it reached Avonwick, supplies of drink were running low, so a stop was made to purchase two cases of whisky from a nearby public house.

A sweepstake was held and the winner allowed to pull the communication cord. This was done south of Gara Bridge and when the train stopped on Topsham level crossing, one of the passengers kindly offered the crossing keeper a glass.

A motorist, surprised at seeing a train stopped away from a station, stepped out of his car to investigate the mystery. He left its engine running and the door open. Arriving at the gate, he was invited on board to join the celebrations. Just as he climbed on, the train left. Dinner was enjoyed on board and the train returned to the crossing three hours later, the car engine still ticking over and the door open. The rest of the party eventually reached Plymouth at forty minutes past midnight.

3

LOCOMOTIVES

A SINGLE-ENDED FAIRLIE

Double-ended narrow-gauge Fairlies with a central cab and boilers at both ends are fairly well known and can be seen on the Ffestiniog Railway working between Portmadoc and Blaenau Ffestiniog. Standard-gauge Fairlies were rare, but one could be seen on the Swindon, Marlborough & Andover Railway and this example was a single-ended type. At first glance it appeared to be an ordinary 0-4-4T, but closer inspection revealed that the driving wheels were not fixed to the frame, but were on a bogie and set far forward.

Its advantage was that it had a greater pulling power than an ordinary engine of the same weight and tractive effort due to the driving wheels being on a bogie, which reduced friction.

In September 1881, Robert Fairlie offered it for trial and, after considering a report by the SMAR's traffic manager, in March 1882 the company offered to buy it for £1,000. Fairlie accepted and after he had received the cheque, forwarded a £30 bill for carriage of the locomotive from Cardiff to Swindon. It became their No. 4.

The flexible steam pipe kept failing. Fairlie proposed a modification and offered to bear half the cost of alteration, a gesture readily accepted. The work was carried out, but in 1884 the locomotive foreman reported: 'No. 4 is little or no use to us for train work, as she can never be depended on and is the most

The Swindon, Marlborough & Andover Railway's Fairlie 0-4-4 tank engine No. 4. She was seen while laid aside at Swindon prior to her overhaul and brief return to service in 1889. The 'Fairlie Patent' plate has become detached and rests on the running board.

expensive engine we have for working.' She burnt 45 to 50 pounds of coal per mile – a heavy consumption for trains of five or six four-wheeled coaches and too heavy for the slender finances of the SMAR.

Possibly the locomotive foreman at Swindon did not fully understand the Walschaert's valve gear and set it incorrectly, because Alexander McDonnell, engineer of the Great Southern & Western Railway in Ireland who built a similar engine, found coal consumption to be 4–5lb per mile less than the average.

No. 4 was kept for reserve use only and acquired the name 'Jumbo', for it was certainly a white elephant. It was involved in an accident in March 1889, which brought the recommendation that continuous brakes should be fitted to passenger trains as soon as possible. Scrapped in 1892, its boiler was retained to supply steam to the company's workshops at Cirencester.

LONG-LASTING LOCOMOTIVE DESIGNS

The GWR had a long tradition of keeping successful designs, incorporating relatively minimal modifications. Daniel Gooch's broad-gauge 4-2-2s of 1847 continued to be built up to 1888, even though they were to have a life of only four years as the broad gauge ended in 1892.

George Churchward brought out his prototype heavy goods 2-8-0 in 1903 and it continued to be built until 1942. In 1952, British Railways, Western Region, made an unsuccessful case for building more and instead was forced to receive BR Standard Class 9 2-10-0s from Crewe. The first GWR 2-8-0 was not withdrawn until 1958, ten years past its official planned life of forty-five years.

The GWR's express counterpart, the 4-6-0 Saint class, also appeared in 1903, but was only built for ten years. In 1924, *Saint Martin* was rebuilt with its 6ft 8½in diameter wheels replaced by those of just 6ft to produce a mixed traffic engine. This became the highly successful Hall class, of which 329 were constructed between 1929 and 1950.

GREAT WESTERN RAILWAY

WOOD-BURNING LOCOMOTIVES

In the 1912 coalminers' strike, due to the scarcity of coal, recourse was made at Paddington to wood burning, the shunting and yard engines there being fed with old sleepers cut into blocks.

SOLIDIFIED OIL FUEL FOR LOCOMOTIVES

In 1912 the Great Western Railway also carried out experiments with solidified oil fuel and used this to maintain a fire after it had been started in the usual way with coal. Queen class 2-2-2 No. 1124 was chosen for the test, hauling trains between Swindon and Didcot and Didcot and Oxford and back. It was not found necessary to modify the engine in any way and, like coal, the fuel was just shovelled into the firebox.

THE CALEDONIAN RAILWAY

ALSO TRIES AN OIL BURNER

During the 1912 miners' strike John McIntosh made experiments with oil-firing on 4-4-0 No. 724, it being adapted so that coal or oil could be used as desired. Oil injection was made by two spraying nozzles placed 18in apart. A cylindrical tank containing 520 gallons of crude oil was placed on the tender. Tests showed that an average train could be hauled on a consumption of 3 gallons, or 27lb, per mile. In addition to the ordinary brick arch, a special firebrick wall was built to protect the copper front plate from the fierce heat of the oil fire.

'OUCH-DEN HALL' – SWINDON DID NOT

GET EVERYTHING RIGHT

By the time the 'Modified Halls' were appearing from the works, the GWR had run out of stately homes for loco names on its own territory and was having to look further afield for inspiration.

No. 6984 *Owsden Hall* is an example, its namesake, which was demolished in 1955, being in west Suffolk between Norwich and Bury St Edmunds. However, it seems there may have been some confusion over the spelling 'Owlsden', meaning 'owl's valley'. It is an historical name for the village usually called Ousden.

The GWR gleaned the names for most of its Halls from three reference books, the first of which was a list of stately homes that opened their gardens to the public occasionally each year, generally to raise money for charity. If a spelling mistake appeared in this book, then it also appeared on the engine. Several more examples or errors can be found in the Manor class: for example No. 7810 *Draycott Manor* should be *Draycot Manor* and No. 7818 *Granville Manor* should have appeared as *Grenville Manor*.

CHANGING THE GAUGE OF LONDON &

NORTH WESTERN RAILWAY LOCOMOTIVES

It was not only broad-gauge Great Western locomotives that had their gauge changed. In 1902, six London & North Western 2-4-2Ts were sold to the Dublin, Wicklow & Wexford Railway. For running over the Irish gauge of 5ft 3in, new axles were fitted at Crewe. The engines were then carried on special wagons to Holyhead and shipped to Dublin.

In 1917, due to a wartime locomotive shortage, these engines were acquired by the government for use at Richborough in connection with the Dunkirk train ferry, so were converted back to standard gauge at Crewe. Subsequently, two of the engines were sold to the Cramlington Colliery Company, Northumberland.

WHITEWASHING

The Edinburgh & Glasgow Railway opened on 18 February 1842. Cowlairs Tunnel, Glasgow, was whitewashed throughout, but by 1843 gas lamps had been placed about 80ft apart alternately on opposite sides of it. A contemporary newspaper wrote: 'By this means the dull, cheerless and to many alarming, feelings which passing through a dark tunnel usually excites will be removed.'

Brunel contended that tunnel lights were unnecessary as a tunnel was no darker than any other part of the line at night.

A LOAD OF NEW ROPE

In the 1840s six carts were linked together and laden with rope for working Cowlairs Incline. The rope was laid in longitudinal coils along all the carts and caused a sensation in the streets of Leith and Edinburgh as they were drawn through the streets; in places nine horses were required to pull the load. The length of the ropes extended to 3 miles, weighed 15 tons and had a diameter of about 2in.

A new haulage cable is being spliced on Cowlairs Incline. In the background are the special brake wagons used to control descending trains. They bear the rather archaic spelling 'break'.

Holmes' 4-4-0 No. 574 enjoys cable assistance up Cowlairs Incline. The hawser is fixed to the hook between the two buffers.

SOMETIMES THE OLD WAY IS BEST

Until 1908 trains descended Cowlairs Incline into Queen Street station, Glasgow, without an engine, but controlled by special brake vans. That year, for trains climbing the gradient of 1 in 42 out of the station, the North British Railway abandoned the stationary steam engine and cable haulage, considering that a modern locomotive, plus a banker at the rear of the train, was capable of taking a train out of Queen Street and also of controlling a train down the incline.

Then, on 12 August 1911, a violent collision occurred at Queen Street when an express from Edinburgh struck the buffers, the engine mounting the platform while coaches were derailed, several passengers receiving serious injury.

A LOCOMOTIVE WORKS ON ONE CYLINDER

On 27 May 1911 the 9 a.m. Southend–Fenchurch Street train was running at almost 60mph between Leigh and Hadley. Suddenly there was a loud rush of steam and clouds of dust and small stones from the ballast enveloped the first part of the train, which stopped abruptly.

The left-hand forward eccentric rod of No. 41 *Leyton* had fractured, the rod thrown off scattering the ballast.

All was not lost. The enginemen disconnected the left-hand side of the engine and then, using just one cylinder, worked the train on to Benfleet at approximately 10mph.

One of the advantages of a steam locomotive was that if a problem arose, its driver could usually do something to get it to a station, whereas with a failed diesel he was generally powerless.

RACEHORSE VERSUS IRON HORSE

In 1842 a curious use was made of the Eastern Counties Railway. A 4-mile steeplechase was run over a course of 2 miles from Romford and back parallel with the railway. To enable the whole race to be seen, a train travelled alongside the steeplechasers from start to finish. The 'excellent arrangements appeared to have given the utmost satisfaction to a very numerous and fashionable company'.

A BELGIAN LOCOMOTIVE

REPAIRED IN ENGLAND

During the First World War, a Belgian State Railway's 0-6-0 was brought for repair at the Stratford Works of the Great Eastern Railway before being sent back to the Western Front.

The locomotive had been constructed in Belgium for the State Railway to the design of John McIntosh, the Caledonian Railway locomotive superintendent.

WATER TROUGH PROBLEM

In 1911 driver Sanderson was travelling along the North Eastern Railway between York and Shildon. At Northallerton he noticed that his engine, 0-8-0 No. 2118, was becoming low on water, but did not stop there as he intended to pick up water on the move at Wiske Moor troughs. When he reached them, he realised that his train was so heavy and slow that insufficient water would be driven into the tender.

A man of initiative, he devised an alternative arrangement. He stopped before the troughs, uncoupled his engine, quickly accelerated for ⅓ mile, filled his tank at the troughs and then reversed to his train before proceeding on his way.

Unfortunately the authorities did not compliment him for his resourcefulness in preventing the main line having the blockage that would have occurred had the shortage of water caused him to throw the fire out, but instead gave him a formal caution.

SNOWED UP

The Highland Railway, due to its geographical location, received more than its fair share of snow storms. A highly dramatic method of clearing snow drifts required three powerful locomotives: one propelling a snow plough and the others coupled behind.

The three engines started from a point about a mile back from the drift blocking the line and in charge of plucky drivers experienced in the work. They were required to accelerate and then dash with terrific force into the obstruction. This was known as 'The Charge' and if successful it scattered the snow on either side of the line, thus securing a clear track, or at least until more drifting occurred.

If an attack was unsuccessful, before a second charge could be made, it was frequently necessary to dig out the plough and locomotives from the mass of snow in which they were wedged.

ON THE FOOTPLATE OF RAILWAY

OPERATING DIVISION ENGINES IN FRANCE

Footplate work in France during in the First World War was a trying experience for the enlisted soldiers. Preparing the engine for the trip was difficult, especially at night when no light could be permitted. Then there were many different types of locomotive to be dealt with: those from various British companies and foreign engines all with different characteristics. There were language problems to contend with and French signals, which were different from the British pattern.

On the military railways there were no fixed signals, only blockmen in cabins working trains on the permissive ticket system. The coal supplied might be bad and unsuitable water cause priming. It was difficult to keep a clean fire on a British engine as they had no drop-bar arrangement as did the French and Belgian machines. Crews could have a continuous turn of sixty hours, and being fourteen days away from a home station was common. After the final push, when the armies were a long way from base, a living van was attached to a train, one crew resting, while the other was on the footplate.

All Railway Operating Division engines were painted black with 'ROD' and the number painted in large white lettering on tender or tank. The first British engines to arrive on the Continent were South Eastern & Chatham Railway 0-6-0Ts employed at Boulogne. London, Brighton & South Coast Railway 0-6-2Ts were employed banking on the hilly section Canaples–Doullens, Great Western Railway 53XX class 2-6-0s also appeared, while 4-6-4Ts built by Beyer, Peacock for the Dutch Railways were appropriated and used in the northern area.

Many British companies supplied 0-6-0s, and North Eastern Railway 0-8-0s were used on roadstone trains. Some 2-8-0s built by the North British Locomotive Company and originally destined for New South Wales worked heavy ammunition trains. These latter engines had long grates and were disliked by those

A Railway Operating Division 2-6-2T locomotive somewhere in France during the First World War.

having to fire them. Belgian engines with no brake at all on the engine and only a hand brake on the tender were abhorred.

British coaches sent out after the Armistice to form demobilisation trains had the British pattern train heating pipe connection and this caused a problem as it would not couple to an engine fitted with the French pattern used on ambulance trains. For those travelling on a demobilisation train for two days, lack of heating was serious.

One ROD driver, J. Birch, commented that the Great Western Railway 53XX class 2-6-0s, of which eleven were sent for ROD use, were the best engines for all-round efficiency, though as he had been a GWR driver, he may have been biased. He said that they had very good brakes and as when running the vacuum pump was worked from the crosshead, this offered a great saving in steam. He observed that the fifty North Eastern Railway 0-8-0s were best for goods trains and that their steam reversing gear was favourably commented on by all who handled them. Of the 0-6-0s, the North British, Great Central and Great Western were the best and those of the Lancashire & Yorkshire unpopular as they were bad steamers and sluggish. North Eastern and North British engines had cabs offering the best shelter, while those of the London & North Western and Great Western offered crews the greatest exposure. The GWR firehole door with two sliding doors worked by one handle was the best pattern and GWR tool boxes on the tender easy to reach; those of other companies less so. Some of the GWR 0-6-0s were fitted with condensing apparatus and carried two additional tanks, one each side of the boiler. All British engines had an arrangement for picking up water from streams, a length of hose being carried. No trouble was experienced in running British engines on the Continental gauge, which was 3/16in wider than the British.

Continental rolling stock being heavier than British and fitted with screw couplings made the use of London & North Western, with their wooden brake blocks and light Caledonian engines, dangerous due to their poor brake power. For goods trains, instead of stopping at the head of an incline for brakes to be pinned down, reliance was placed on the guard in a van next to the engine and his two or more brakesmen riding in small huts attached to a large proportion of the French rolling stock, who each applied the brake from his seat.

Driver Birch expressed surprise that the responsible authorities permitted the brass domes on the Dutch engines and the copious brasswork on Belgian engines to be polished brightly, because when working near the front they were often in view of Germans in spotter balloons and thus attracted attention. He found it interesting that stations in France had no bridges or subways provided for crossing the line safely, so at large stations trains were usually divided until ready to depart in order to enable passengers to cross to other platforms.

ANOTHER ROD DRIVER COMMENTS ON

DRIVER BIRCH'S RECOLLECTIONS

Robert Walker, an ROD driver from the Caledonian Railway, said he believed that although the GWR 53XX class 2-6-0s were, in general efficiency, equal to Robinson's War Department 2-8-0s when running on the level, they were less so on an incline. He also found them rough-riding and with a marked oscillation at high speed.

Regarding the GWR 0-6-0s, the chalky water found in France caused the ball check valve of their ordinary injector to continually fur up and believed the best class of 0-6-0 to be those of the Belgian State Railway. As to the Caledonian Railway engines being 'dangerous', he claimed that they were very good engines for construction work, being light on water and more powerful than the majority of 0-6-0s.

When the water-lifting apparatus was used to raise water from such places as shell holes, the water was often dirty, causing gauge cocks to be blocked and injector cones to fur. As the injector on a London & North Western Railway engine was placed under the footplate, it was impossible to tell if an injector was working and filling the boiler; thus many fireboxes were burnt through the shortage of water and men punished due to circumstances over which they had no control.

HEARING A DETONATOR

The driver of the train involved in the Caledonian Railway's Kirtlebridge collision of 19 December 1917 stated that he did not hear the noise of the exploding detonator, which would have warned him of the danger.

This incident led the London & South Western Railway to carry out experiments with 4-4-0 No. 441 to ensure that the result of an explosion was carried to the cab. The noise entered the mouthpiece of an apparatus and reached a pneumatic chamber, which broke an electrical circuit giving a visual indication in the cab of red and white, the sounding of an electric bell and making a brake application. These warnings continued until the driver, or drivers as it also sounded on a second engine if present, reset the apparatus.

Although a good idea, it was not adopted as, in normal circumstances, a driver was audibly aware of a detonator exploding.

AN UNLUCKY LOCOMOTIVE

English Electric Class 40 D326 involved in the Great Train Robbery of 8 August 1963 was an unlucky locomotive, as it was involved in other accidents and mishaps. On 26 December 1962, when hauling the Midday Scot, due to a driver's error it struck the rear of the 16.45 Liverpool–Birmingham express between Winsford and Coppenhall Junction, Cheshire, killing eighteen passengers. Then, in 1964, a fireman was killed when climbing on its nose to clean the windscreen and touched the overhead electric wires. In 1965, it was approaching Birmingham New Street when the brakes failed and only quick thinking by a signalman diverted it to another platform. There it struck the rear of a freight train but only the guard was injured and a serious crash was avoided.

GERMANS CAPTURE A MIDLAND
RAILWAY ENGINE

When the Germans made a sudden breakthrough in the Allied line at Cambrai in 1917, Midland Railway Kirtley 0-6-0 No. 2717 was in a forward area, and when the fighting subsided was stuck a few hundred yards behind the new front-line trenches.

LOCOMOTIVES

Troops were able to remove the wagons of its train one by one at nights using a petrol tractor, the infantry putting up a barrage to cover the sound of the removal. However, it was impossible to remove the engine under her own steam, even had it been possible to raise steam, which it was not due to the fact that she was riddled with bullets. The tractor was unable to move her.

In the German push of spring 1918 she was captured by the Germans, who got her in running order and used her to help them fight the war. During the Allied push in the autumn of 1918, she was recaptured by the Belgians and, following the Armistice, eventually found her way back to the Midland Railway and placed in service on that line.

A HORSE TAKES A FREE RIDE

The *Stratford-upon-Avon Herald* of 3 June 1904 recounted events that took place in about 1877 when the Shipston branch was worked by a horse named Jumper:

At the head of a steep gradient we pull up. The driver gets off, unhooks Jumper out of the traces, brings him round to the rear of the truck, and shunts a pebble against the front wheel. Jumper seemed to be putting himself into position for something. All at once Saunders let the tail-board down, and to my amazement Jumper bolted up into the truck with the agility of a cat.

Says Bill Saunders, 'Don't you stir an inch, Mister Phelps. As soon as I a' shifted the pebble and put the points right, we shall begin to move.' Afterwards he gave it a push. All at once our truck began to move at a snail's pace. Saunders jumped on to the nearside, I was on the off-side, and Jumper was in the middle of the truck, with his head high up in the air. The truck began to go a bit faster. Jumper put his forelegs out an inch or two, so as to get a better standing. We were now going at a fast pace down the incline. Jumper stood up as firm as Ilmington church tower.

All at once in the distance we saw impediments on the line. Saunders found his brake wouldn't act in consequence of our terrific speed. We got near enough to see it was a farmer with a donkey and cart, and a calf in it a-baaing, and her mother the cow was jumping about on the line after her calf, and the farmer was trying to get donkey, cart and calf down the embankment, but the moke wouldn't stir an inch. The crash was coming when all at once Farmer Cropper of Darlingscott was equal to the occasion. He lifted the tail of the donkey and away went the donkey, cart and calf down the embankment.

We entered Shipston in good style. After the tail-board of our truck was let down, Jumper twisted round, and jumped out of the truck like a cat.

TROUBLE WITH THE WIND

It is not always realised that the wind affects the speed of a train. Strong headwinds offer the greatest resistance, but side winds, especially with long trains, have a considerable effect, while a following wind helps progress.

GETTING THEIR OWN BACK

Some of the London & North Western Railway's 4-6-0 Claughton-class locomotives were named after directors.

One day a train was too heavy for one Claughton to pull. It happened to be named after a director not in favour with the locomotive staff so they made a point by placing another Claughton, named *Vindictive*, in front.

SUPERSTITIOUS?

In 1918, West Cumberland was clearly not superstitious because three engines with the number thirteen were seen daily in that area. London & North Western Railway 0-6-2T No. 13 worked goods and passenger trains Whitehaven–Maryport; Furness Railway 0-6-0 No. 13 headed goods trains from Cleator Moor–Carlisle via Maryport, while the Maryport & Carlisle Railway 2-4-0 No. 13 worked the 5.25 p.m. passenger train Maryport–Barrow. Additionally, Furness Railway No. 113 headed a train Workington–Maryport.

A HORSE-POWERED LOCOMOTIVE

In 1850 an Italian, Clemente Masserano, interested the London & South Western Railway directors in a cheap form of locomotive named *Impulsoria*. Basically it was a 2-2-0 locomotive frame with an endless belt on which four horses trotted. The motion of the platform was passed through gearing and thence to a pulley on the trailing wheels by a rope drive. One excellent feature was that its axles had roller bearings. Its advantage was that horses cost 2*s* 0*d* a day, whereas steam locomotives used 6*d* worth of coal per mile. *Impulsoria* could draw thirty wagons up the incline at Nine Elms Goods Depot. None were ordered as it was considered a mere scientific novelty.

BELT AND BRACES

In Scotland the Newtyle & Coupar Angus and Newtyle & Glamis Railways used sail propulsion for its passenger coach, speeds up to 20mph being reached. A horse was available when the wind dropped.

THE LONGEST JOURNEY MADE IN

GREAT BRITAIN BY LOCOMOTIVES OF

A PRE-GROUPING COMPANY

In 1913 this was 405½ miles on the Great Western Railway:

	Miles
Penzance–Bristol	207
Bristol–Birmingham	98¾
Birmingham–Birkenhead	99¾

Only one change of train was made and this was at Birmingham, Snow Hill. The time taken for the journey was twelve hours seven minutes.

LIFE-SAVING FIREMAN

Early in 1914, a Down London & North Western Railway goods train was approaching Carlisle and running alongside the River Petteril. The fireman was leaning out of the cab the more easily to observe the signals. He spotted a man lying on the river bank with his head and shoulders in the water and told his driver, who immediately stopped the train. The fireman hurried back and found the man apparently dead. He had attended first-aid courses, so attempted artificial respiration and had the great satisfaction of seeing the patient recover.

Meanwhile, the driver had taken his train on alone the few miles to Carlisle and arranged for medical assistance to be sent, whereupon the man was found sufficiently recovered to be escorted home. The mishap had occurred because he lost his footing on the bank, was unable to grasp anything to pull himself out of the water and thus quite helpless until the fireman came to his rescue.

STRAWBERRIES AND GOLD

Sir William Portal, deputy chairman of the London & South Western Railway, speaking at the annual dinner of the Bournemouth Central station staff produced the following statistics:

On 23 June 1913 the Swanwick and Fareham district despatched 46,730 baskets of strawberries – a total of 93 tons that day. Some 610,200 baskets of strawberries weighing 1,220 tons were sent in the season of four weeks;

A total of 31,900 packets of gold and silver bullion weighing 11,000 tons were carried by the company that year.

Carts arrive at Botley with strawberries *c.* 1905. Rolling stock is in such short supply that four-wheeled passenger coaches have had to be pressed into service to carry the fruit.

SPENDING A PENNY

A curious point was raised at a Licensing Sessions at Blackburn in 1914 as to whether a railway company had the right to charge one penny admission to a platform to someone who wished to make use of the bar of the station refreshment room, because no other licensed house was allowed to make such a charge.

On the other hand, people were willing to spend a penny on a platform ticket to pose as a traveller in order to obtain refreshment at a railway station during the hours that the licensed premises were closed to non-travellers.

HUMOROUS LOCOMOTIVE NAMES

In 1836 the 0-2-2T *Surprise*, designed by Dr William Church of Birmingham, was somewhat of a curiosity. It had a vertical boiler and its footplate set at the front between the two cylinders, the crew having no protection from the weather. It was tried by the London & Birmingham and Grand Junction companies and then languished for a time on a siding in Birmingham; so long, in fact, that rain had entered through the uncapped chimney and rusted away some of the boiler plating.

On 3 November 1840, the Birmingham & Gloucester Railway agreed to find the fuel for a month's test. On the evening of 10 November, after making several short trips, it lived up to its name when the thin boiler plates burst with a tremendous explosion, killing driver Thomas Scaife and injuring locomotive foreman Joseph Rutherford so badly that he died the next day.

Repaired and renamed *Eclipse*, the engine was offered to the Birmingham & Gloucester for a trial on 30 August 1842, but unsurprisingly the proposal was declined.

The Great Western Railway had a locomotive named *Load Star*, not due to its excellent tractive effort, or to the spelling ignorance of the nineteenth-century workforce, but to the fact

This Great Western Railway 2-4-0 named *Avonside* was originally given the rather unfortunate name *Slaughter*.

that this was an older spelling of *Lode Star*, which the engine was eventually renamed.

Four extremely ugly-looking, lumbering, broad-gauge goods engines were named respectively *Cupid*, *Coquette*, *Flirt* and *Flora* – perhaps in an effort to try and make them more attractive? In a way, one name was used twice, as 'coquette' is the French for 'flirt'.

In 1865–66 twenty broad-gauge engines were named after eminent locomotive engineers – and one was named *Slaughter*. One day a GWR director travelled in a train hauled by *Slaughter* and, believing it could be thought an ill omen by nervous passengers, brought the matter to the attention of the board of directors. They amended it to *Avonside* – the name of Slaughter's locomotive works.

Some rather angular GWR engines built in 1908 were named after flowers – perhaps to help soften their outlines.

A 4-4-0 County-class engine was named *County of Cheshire* – a tautological expression that, when pointed out, was amended after six months to *County of Chester.* The GWR did not learn the lesson and, when in post-Second World War years a new 4-6-0 County class appeared, one was about to be named *County of Cheshire,* but the mistake was spotted and corrected before the nameplate was mounted.

A London & North Western engine was named *Liver* after the bird from which Liverpool derives its name. Liverpudlians are careful to pronounce *Liver* with a long 'i', but unfortunately the locomotive was for many years shedded in the Midlands and the natives of that district knew nothing and cared less about Liverpool's pet bird. Hence, they pronounced it as if it was named after a part of the human anatomy.

Two names, perhaps taken from Euclid's treatise on geometry, were the London & North Western's *Problem* and *Theorem.* A non-mathematical passenger seeing his train arriving at the platform headed by a locomotive named *Problem* might have been apprehensive as to whether his journey would be completed safely.

The railway historian E.L. Ahrons relates that it was a fact that Francis Webb, the LNWR locomotive superintendent, once gave his young engineers a moral lecture using the names of three of his engines: *Pluck, Patience* and *Perseverance.*

A locomotive named *Dachshund* conveys to most people an engine with an enormously long boiler and very small wheels, but it was in fact a fine express engine that waddled from Euston to Crewe at 60mph. A first cousin to *Dachshund* was the GWR Star-class 4-6-0 *King Charles,* though some learned authorities contended that the engine was named after the dog's owner.

Another LNWR engine, *Psyche,* was a difficult name for some its crews to pronounce, so they unofficially referred to it as *Physic.*

The London, Brighton & South Coast named many of their engines after stations on the line. One was named *Crawley,* but to an anxious passenger, late for an appointment, it may have suggested the speed of the train. Other lines, such as the Great

Western and London, Tilbury & Southend, also named engines after stations. These names were occasionally sources of trouble when some passengers mistook them for destination boards!

Most of the GWR Hall-class 4-6-0s were named after stately homes, but several, such as *Colston Hall* and *Albert Hall*, were named after entertainment centres. *Toynbee Hall* was the name of a charitable foundation, not even a building. Fortunately, the GWR did not name one *Henry Hall* after the dance band leader!

The Southern Railway had a class of locomotives named after public schools. A witty enthusiast, seeing the name *Arrow* affixed to the smoke-deflector plates of a British Railways Standard Class 7 4-6-2, said, 'Look! A Schools class engine.'

HORSE - STEAM - HORSE

It was a curious fact that before the Grouping in 1923, Scottish railways had lines in England, but no English railway had any lines in Scotland.

One English branch that the Scottish North British Railway owned was the Port Carlisle line. It was so called due to its location on the Solway Firth being the nearest Carlisle could be reached by any vessel of moderate tonnage.

A canal linked the port with the city and in 1854 this was turned into a railway worked by locomotives. Due to its ancestry, it ran in cuttings for much of its length, with sudden steep gradients where locks had been sited.

With the silting of the Solway Firth, shipping at Port Carlisle declined and the economically minded directors of the NBR decided that working by steam locomotives was too expensive and so introduced horse power, a suitable animal being purchased for £35. The canny Scots had done the right thing, for it was estimated that in the first quarter of 1858 the horse had saved 1,887 engine miles. Following stage coach tradition, first-class passengers sat inside and third-class outside. By 1899, the track was in such poor

The North British Railway's Port Carlisle 'dandy' seen *c*. 1910. The notice on the door reads: 'For first and second class passengers only' – the third class had to sit outside.

condition that it was not safe for use by locomotives, and so goods wagons were horse-drawn too.

Immediately prior to the First World War, the Port Carlisle district attracted tourists and an increase in traffic caused the directors to rethink, with the result that a 0-6-0T and two coaches replaced the horse service on 6 April 1914. The first train on the newly introduced steam service carried horseboxes conveying the superseded 'locomotives' literally to 'fresh fields and pastures new'.

The passenger coach known as a Dandy car was recycled as a pavilion by a local bowling club, but in 1925 was recovered by the London & North Eastern Railway for the Stockton & Darlington Railway centenary celebrations. It is now in the National Railway Museum, York.

1842 ELECTRIC LOCOMOTIVE

In 1842 an electro-magnetic locomotive invented by Mr Davidson was tried in the carriage sheds of the Edinburgh & Glasgow Railway. Although its progress was slow and accompanied by blinding flashes, its possibilities were recognised.

Current was provided from batteries consisting of zinc and iron corrugated plates immersed in dilute sulphuric acid. This drove a simple motor working on the principle of the attraction of iron bars on a revolving cylinder, to fixed electro-magnets, energised and de-energised at intervals by a commutator and brush.

The locomotive, 16ft in length and 7ft wide, weighed 6 tons and was carried on four 3ft-diameter wheels. It travelled for 1½ miles at 4mph until the battery became exhausted and required emptying and filling with new acid.

RACING CORRESPONDENTS

Before the invention of the electric telegraph made it easy to send messages rapidly over long distances, the national newspapers chartered an engine to carry important despatches. For instance, during the French Revolution in 1848, the *Times* and the *Herald* each paid a retaining fee of £5 a day and £5 a night just for an engine to stand at Folkestone to convey to London a despatch-bearer from Paris. Both papers also paid an additional £30 for the journey to London and the special correspondents raced each other from the ferry landing stage to the first engine. They refused to share a train, a driver remarking: 'If one of them got his foot on the engine, 'twas his train, and he wouldn't wait for a carriage. One day the *Herald* man reached the engine first and the *Times* man was terribly annoyed as he was usually the winner. 'I'll give £3,' said he to the driver of the second engine, 'if you can get in front of him.'

This seemed an impossible task since both trains used the same track to London, but the driver continued: 'I took water before I came to Tonbridge and when he was taking in water in the siding there, I got in front of him and won the money.'

Today we enjoy the instant electronic communication of news from all over the world, so newspapers are not so important, but in the early days of railways, they were a highly valued source of information. Local newspapers were usually only published weekly, but London ones appeared daily.

The date 19 February 1848 was a red-letter day in the history of the London press as the first special newspaper train from the metropolis enabled London papers to reach the chief cities in the North of England before noon, and they were in the hands of Glasgow and Edinburgh readers by the afternoon.

In 1848 the country was anxious about Lord John Russell's budget proposals to be laid before Parliament on 19 February. W.H. Smith, newsagent, had the brilliant idea of arranging with the railway companies to distribute the London papers containing the budget reports and debates, but these could not be printed until the early hours of 20 February. Until 15 February the railway route to Scotland was the London & North Western Euston–Rugby, from where the Midland and its associates took the passengers on through York, Newcastle, Edinburgh and Glasgow. It was not quite railway track throughout as river bridges at Newcastle and Berwick were incomplete and road transport had to be used for a short distance.

With the opening of the Caledonian Railway Carlisle–Glasgow and Edinburgh on 15 February, the West Coast route was complete. Smith's idea was to charter two trains: one to Glasgow via the West Coast and the other to Edinburgh via York, but the Caledonian declined as its line was not in proper order, so just one train ran to Scotland via York.

It left Euston at 5.35 a.m. and reached Glasgow at 3.57 p.m. Traversing the road sections Gateshead–Newcastle and Tweedmouth–Berwick took only eight and seven minutes respectively.

A LOCOMOTIVE AIDS A SHIP IN DISTRESS

The east coast of England experienced devastating floods in 1953. One disaster was when the supports of two vessels in dry dock at Immingham were washed away and, having nothing to keep them upright, they toppled over. In due course, water was pumped out of the ships which still lay on their sides.

The solution was highly imaginative. Steel pillars were welded to the hulls, steel hawsers attached and passed through pulley blocks that magnified the pull fourteen times. Two Eastern Region O4 class 2-8-0 locomotives were driven to a line beside the dock. They slowly pulled on the rope as water was admitted to the dry dock and in about thirty minutes the first ship was vertical again. The second vessel was dealt with in a similar fashion.

THE PWLLYRHEBOG INCLINE

One length of line on the Taff Vale Railway had a gradient of 1 in 13 for ½ mile. It was known as the Pwllyrhebog Incline and even if the gradient had not been severe, the spelling, let alone the pronunciation of its name, was enough to frighten anyone save a native Welsh speaker.

Worked as a balanced incline, it varied from others as to avoid breakaways an engine pushed wagons up the incline, the rope passing below the train to connect with the engine.

In 1884 the locomotive superintendent, T.H. Riches, designed three engines specially to work this Pwllyrhebog Incline. They were 0-6-0Ts, and to improve braking capacity, a shoe brake was fitted between the driving and trailing wheels. An engine normally worked up the incline bunker-first, to ensure that the top of the firebox was adequately covered by water. Generally two engines worked the incline with the third kept as a spare. Each engine worked for a month followed by a fortnight's rest.

The Taff Vale Railway H-class incline locomotive No. 143 used on its Pwllyrhebog line. It became Great Western Railway No. 794, British Railways No. 195 and was withdrawn in November 1951.

The three locomotives survived the 1923 Grouping to become GWR property and then BR in 1948, soon after the incline being closed and the engines sold to the National Coal Board. In view of the fact that the branch was short, it is surprising that over the sixty-seven years they were employed on their original duty, Taff Vale No. 141 (GWR No. 792/193) achieved 943,197 miles.

The steepness of the incline demanded that locomotives working it had a special type of boiler – a taper-boiler that allowed water to be always over the top of the firebox when on a slope. For the same reason, the dome was on the firebox and not the boiler barrel. The Taff Vale introduced the taper boiler before the Great Western Railway adopted it.

Although the incline was double tracked, the roads were not designated Up and Down, but left-hand and right-hand. This was because a locomotive propelled a train up in order to guard against runaways, while a descending train had a locomotive at the front to act as a brake. A wire rope passing over a drum at the top linked the two engines, the drum controlled by a brake. An indicator showed the train speed and if in excess of 5mph, brakes were applied to the drum. The maximum load up was ten empties, or five loaded with pit props; the down maximum load was ten loaded wagons.

Safety points at the top were interlocked with the signal controlling the downward movement, while at the foot of the incline was a runaway siding. The points were set for this siding and were not moved until the train was safely at a standstill at the foot of the inclined plane.

A bankrider travelled on all down trains and applied the wagons' brakes before a train started and was required to ride on one of the wagons from top to bottom.

At one time, c. 1910 to c. 1932, to offer more flexible working, three old tenders coupled together were kept at the top of the incline to act as a counterbalance for ascending trains in order for a train at the bottom to proceed without having to wait until a loaded train had been assembled at the summit. A bankrider was required to ride on these tenders.

A white post marked the spot at the foot of the incline where the locomotive must stop to prevent the possibility of the counterbalance being drawn over the head of the incline. When two tenders replaced the second locomotive, the maximum up load was reduced to eight empties, or four loaded with pit props, and eight laden wagons in the down direction, but in bad weather a driver could require a smaller load.

OLDHAM INCLINE

Another fascinating incline was the ¼ mile of 1 in 27 at Oldham. From the opening of the line in 1843, ascending trains had a rope attached to the engine. It passed over a wheel at the top and the other end coupled to a descending train, which also had a locomotive. Soon an economy was practised by the balancing train simply consisting of a heavy brake van and wagons filled with sand. One set of rails was kept solely for the counterbalance, goods or passenger trains using the other set. Passenger trains ascended at about 25mph, the descending speed being the same.

When a colliery opened at the summit, loaded coal wagons were used as a counterbalance instead of sand, allowing income to be obtained from the counterbalance.

The rope weighed 6 tons 6cwt and lasted an average of two years four months. From 1856 the design of locomotives had developed sufficiently for them to haul and bank trains up the gradient, so rope working was abolished.

HEALTH & SAFETY NIGHTMARE

In 1842 four-wheel engines were believed to be less safe than those with six wheels as it was thought that if the front axle of a two-axle locomotive broke a serious accident would occur.

Edward Bury, locomotive manufacturer and designer of London & Birmingham Railway engines, favoured the four-wheel design and conducted what today would be considered a risky experiment on No. 18.

The front axle was cut near a journal so that it was only an inch wide at the incision. The engine then travelled from Wolverton towards Roade, 7¼ miles distant, until, as intended, the axle snapped. The engine returned to Wolverton and collected six loaded wagons and started with the front wheels loose and only held in position by the journals. It travelled the 34 miles to Watford at 25mph, whereupon one of the front wheels slipped off the rail and the train was delayed for seven minutes while the engine was replaced on the track. Two miles south of Harrow the engine again derailed and then arrived at Camden without further mishap. It was said that this proved that two-axle locomotives were as safe as those with three axles.

THERE ARE SAINTS AND SAINTS

It is not always realised that there were two classes of Great
Western Railway 'Saints'. There were the 4-6-0 Saint-class
locomotives with such names as *Saint Agatha*, *Saint George* etc,
and there were eleven 4-4-0 engines of the Duke and Bulldog
classes such as *St Agnes* and *St Ives* named after places in Cornwall
and with 'Saint' written in its abbreviated form.

NAMERS

At one time the London, Brighton & South Coast Railway
had almost all of its engines named – 520 out of a total of
approximately 600 – with only the large tender goods engines
remaining unnamed. When D. Earle Marsh was appointed
locomotive superintendent in 1905 most of the names were
omitted when the engines were repainted. He had come from the
Great Northern Railway, which had a no-name policy. This move
made the LBSCR passengers sad and they thought back longingly
to the times of spotlessly clean yellow engines distinguished by
names that for thirty-five years had characterised the line from
the time of William Stroudley, the gilt letters shaded with green.

Although most of the names were those of stations in LBSCR
territory, some were of continental origin and the sight of an
engine bearing the name *Cannes* or *Genoa* on a damp, foggy
London morning was an inspiration. A few other LBSCR engines
were named after men in the public eye.

The London, Tilbury & Southend Railway also had all of
its engines named except for a couple of large goods engines.
Although the LTSR chose local names, not all were melodious
– *Black Horse Road*, *Commercial Road* and *Dagenham Dock*
almost giving ridicule rather than added interest to the stock
of fine locomotives. When the Midland Railway took over the
company, the names disappeared, as named engines on the MR

London, Brighton & South Coast Railway No. 8 *Boxhill* in the short-lived British Transport Museum, Clapham Common.

were rare. Similarly, London & South Western engines were unnamed latterly except for the Southampton Dock tank engines. It was a pity that the Furness Railway did not name engines as it had delightful-sounding possibilities in its area: Windermere, Grasmere and Silverdale.

It behoved every railway company to make travel over its line an experience that would leave a feeling of interest. A company which named its locomotives, had attractive stations, maintained its permanent way as finely as a drive to a country mansion and its hedges as those of a well-kept garden was the company that would always have traffic.

Generally, a single name seemed to suit an engine better than a full name – the London, Brighton & South Coast's *Siemens*, *Bessemer* and *Trevithick* were more melodious and flew off the tongue more readily than *William Siemens, Henry Bessemer* and *Richard Trevithick* of the London & North Western.

QUEEN VICTORIA'S DIAMOND JUBILEE

To celebrate Queen Victoria's Diamond Jubilee in 1897, the London & North Western Railway's No. 2053 *Greater Britain* was painted in brilliant vermilion and No. 2054 *Queen Empress* creamy-white picked out with red. They were particularly striking as the LNWR standard livery was black. No LNWR blue engine appeared to complete the trio of patriotic colours, but as Caledonian Railway engines were blue, the Queen's motive power on her summer journey to Balmoral would have been suitably patriotic in hue.

Greater Britain was repainted in standard livery in July 1898, but with the addition of a thick red lining.

On the death of Prime Minister William Gladstone, LNWR No. 1521 *Gladstone* had its buffer beams and number plate painted black instead of the usual red.

LOCOMOTIVE STANDARDISATION

In 1918 a Committee of Railway Locomotive Engineers and Carriage and Wagon Superintendents considered the advantages and disadvantages of standardisation of rolling stock. Due to the very varying structure gauges of British railways and the different carrying capacity of bridges owned by the various companies, to have made locomotives, carriages and wagons of such dimensions to enable them to travel anywhere would have been a retrograde policy rather than a progressive one. Those railways that had increased their carrying capacity per train mile would have been forced to revert to smaller and less efficient plant in order to make it suitable to travel universally.

Regarding locomotives, Sir John Aspinall, of the Lancashire & Yorkshire, said it was often necessary to have more than one class of a certain type of locomotive: for instance, a 4-4-0 express passenger locomotive designed for hauling long-distance passenger trains may be quite unsuitable for working stopping trains, so a different class would be necessary for this task, though many of the working parts could be the same.

Aspinall believed that a large railway company would need at least seven types: an express passenger tender engine; an ordinary passenger tender engine; a passenger tank engine for local and express trains; fast goods engine; heavy mineral engine; powerful shunting engine and a shunting engine for light work.

HAPPY-GO-LUCKY

One day in 1842 the secretary of the London & Greenwich Railway missed an Up train so he mounted an engine, which then chased the train he had failed to catch. The driver of that train, seeing an engine chasing him, slackened speed to allow it to catch up, but the driver of the light engine failed to reduce speed. When it was realised that a collision was inevitable, the last carriage was detached in order to limit damage to that coach alone. Fortunately its passengers were only bruised and shaken.

PRAISE INDEED FOR BRITISH

LOCOMOTIVES

Robert E. Thayer, European editor of the American publication *Railway Age*, wrote in 1920:

The English locomotives are very small when compared with the more modern locomotives used in this country, but do their work with an apparent lack of effort that is particularly noteworthy. They are well-proportioned and particularly well-kept. The expression that they are 'built like a watch' is hardly an exaggeration. The weight is so carefully distributed on the wheels that no equalisation is found necessary. With such care taken in the construction, it will be readily understood that they do not suffer any great maintenance troubles. These are further alleviated by the excellent roadbed found in England. The riding qualities of the locomotives can well be surmised. The writer had the privilege of riding a Midland 4-4-0 engine which had been out of the shops for eighteen months and exceeded its mileage. But its riding qualities were far superior to any of the most perfectly maintained locomotives in the States and would compare favourably with the riding qualities of a good many of the coaches on some of our trains at the present time.

ELECTRIC BATTERY PROPULSION

– THE LATEST FAD IN 1913

Electric battery propulsion for road vehicles is part of the latest effort to combat global warming, but it is not a twenty-first-century idea: the Midland Railway adopted it more than a century ago. In 1913, J. Dalziel, the company's chief electrical engineer's assistant, designed a battery locomotive for shunting to replace five horses and four men. By 1920 its annual working cost was £400, or £800 including provision for battery renewal, interest and depreciation, whereas the cost of the horses and men would have been £1,600; thus it had saved the company £800 annually.

About the same date, the North Staffordshire Railway also constructed a battery-powered shunter at its Stoke Locomotive Works.

It was a joint design of J.A. Hookham and A.F. Rock, the locomotive superintendent and electrical engineer respectively. The four-wheeled engine had a motor on each axle and weighed 17 tons, the weight of the battery being 6 tons 8cwt of the total. On the level it could haul 90 tons at 10mph, or 72 tons at 11mph.

FOWLER'S GHOST

When London's first underground railway was planned, it was realised that tunnels full of smoke would not endear the system to passengers, so a smokeless locomotive was designed by the Metropolitan Railway's chief engineer, John Fowler. Its fire heated firebricks and when these were hot, the fire was allowed to die down, the firebricks retaining heat and allowing the boiler still to generate steam. This 2-2-2T was known as Fowler's Ghost, but when tested on the Great Western Railway's main line it ran out of steam after only 7½ miles: like King Alfred's hot cakes, Sir John's hot bricks were a failure.

Daniel Gooch, the GWR's locomotive engineer, provided something more suitable. This was a 2-4-0 well tank fitted with condensing apparatus, flaps sending exhaust steam up the chimney when working in the open, but directed into the water tanks when in a tunnel. These were the very first condensing locomotives in Britain and the only broad-gauge engines Gooch built with outside cylinders.

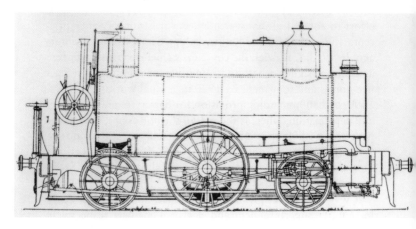

'Fowler's Ghost', a smokeless locomotive built in 1861 by Robert Stephenson & Co. It used pre-heated fire-bricks.

The GWR and the Metropolitan Railway did not always see eye to eye, so the GWR withdrew its engines after working the line for seven months. They proved not very successful when worked on the GWR's ordinary services and seven of the twenty-two were converted to tender engines. When the class was withdrawn after only about ten years' work, all the boilers were used for stationary work, one sold to the Telegraph Construction Company for use on the SS *Great Eastern*.

THE GOVERNMENT KNOWS BEST

The magazine *Transport & Travel* for May 1922 revealed:

From time to time the government sanctions the spending of hundreds of thousands, or it may be millions of money upon schemes that a boy selling newspapers in the street would at once recognise as useless.

The building of locomotives at Woolwich Arsenal is a case of this character.

The Government seeks to excuse the waste on the following grounds:-

At the time of the Armistice, the number of employees at Woolwich was far in excess of the normal peacetime establishment. The government had either to discharge the surplus men or else try and obtain alternative work for them. It was not at this time possible to obtain alternative work to any large extent for definite orders. It was therefore decided to adopt some kind of work which they thought would result in their being able to balance expenditure by the sale of the goods manufactured. It was determined that they should embark on building locomotives, and 100 were ordered. This work was still not completed, and up to now [May 1922] there were still no purchasers. The government did their best to sell those that were ready during the past year, but without success.

After 3½ years work, 40 of the engines have been finished. They have cost £16,000 each. The highest price asked for similar engines by private builders during the shortage of 1919–20 was only £12,000 each, including builder's profit, or £4,000 each less than for the Government to build without allowing anything for profit.

Similar engines can now be bought for about £9,000 each, so that unless the Government will accept this price for them, it is impossible to sell them. Meanwhile, there is still £880,000 wanted to complete the remaining 55 of the hundred.

What is the use of continuing the waste of money by completing the engines? Work should be stopped at once, and the engines finished and unfinished, handed over to the railways, at market – not cost price and brought into account in the settlement of outstanding liabilities arising out of the Government control of the railways.

4

WORKFORCE

THE BIG BANG

Between Gloucester and Bristol is the 1,400yd Wickwar Tunnel. Finishing work at midday on Saturday, the foreman was concerned that the gunpowder would become wet and useless. Where could a warm and dry place be found? The blacksmith's shop seemed ideal.

Unfortunately the blacksmith was not informed of the move, and when he started work on Monday, a spark flew out from a pick he was sharpening …!

THE MYSTERY OF THE MISSING DRIVER

On 18 December 1899 the 6.50 p.m. from Weymouth to Portland was crossing Backwater Viaduct. Fireman Willis was busy attending to his fire and a little later looked over the side of the cab to allow his eyes to adjust to the dark so that he could observe the Rodwell signals. On approaching them, he wondered why the engine was going so slowly. About to question his driver, he was amazed to discover he was no longer on the footplate.

Willis stopped the train at the platform and, believing that Driver Nutman had fallen off, the line back to Weymouth was carefully searched but no trace of him was found. A spare driver worked the last two trips of the day with Fireman Willis.

The Backwater Viaduct where Driver Nutman leaped off his engine can be seen beyond Melcombe Regis station.

The following day, Driver Nutman's cap was found on Backwater Viaduct. It was assumed he had fallen in and drowned, so the area was dragged in an effort to locate the body. Nothing was brought up.

Mrs Nutman made inquiries and in February 1900 reported to the Weymouth shedmaster that her husband had been seen in Shepton Mallet, Somerset, with her younger sister, who had disappeared from her home. The police discovered the couple living in a village near Leatherhead, where he was working as a woodcutter.

Nutman was arrested and stood trial at Dorchester Assizes in July 1900 charged with 'unlawfully and wilfully leaving an engine whereby the lives and persons of those travelling along the Great Western & South Western Portland Joint Railway might have been endangered'. Found guilty, he was given six months' hard labour in Dorchester Gaol. (It transpired that he had jumped off the engine on Backwater Viaduct.)

FIREMAN AT RISK

While shovelling coal into the firebox of a London & North Western Railway engine heading a goods train in the Sirhowy Valley, Monmouthshire, the fireman discovered, among the coal in the tender, a cartridge similar to those used for blasting in collieries. As he held it in his left hand, the cartridge exploded, blowing off his forefinger and thumb, also injuring his right hand and face. However, had he not spotted the cartridge before shovelling it into the firebox, the resultant explosion could have killed both him and his driver.

THE LLANELLY RAILWAY AND ITS
UNUSUAL PRACTICES

The Llanelly Railway comprised 46 miles of single track and was not worked with a train staff as would be expected, but used the speaking telegraph. 'Is line clear?' would receive the answer 'Yes', and 'Train leaving' would receive the answer 'Good'.

On its mineral branches, trains were usually worked with no brake vans, the brakesmen placing a flag or tree branch on the last wagon so that a driver could look back and see that his train was complete.

The mineral branches were worked by an unusual method. The engine and one brakesman ran well in front of the train itself and at each colliery collected the wagons requiring despatch and left them on the main line to be picked up by the other brakesman, the engineless train proceeding behind under gravity. When sufficient wagons had been assembled, the engine was coupled on, one brakesman riding on the buffers and, in an emergency, running alongside the wagons dropping their brakes.

HOW RAILWAY COMPANIES ENCOURAGED

FOOD PRODUCTION IN THE

FIRST WORLD WAR

To help ease the food shortage during in the First World War caused by German submarines torpedoing ships bringing imports to Britain, railwaymen were encouraged to have allotments beside the line.

Some were set up at Nine Elms Goods yard and, with enthusiasm that did them credit, London & South Western railwaymen developed a portion of the yard near the former locomotive works after clearing the 'soil' of sundry decayed sleepers, scrap iron and broken bricks before growing potatoes and other produce. The *South Western Railway Magazine* stated dryly: 'It is recorded that the Nine Elms sparrows are chirping more brightly than usual in pleasant anticipation of a good time coming.'

LSWR men worked some 6,000 allotments, the company letting the men have free use of the land beside the line, while the directors offered prizes for exhibits at railway garden shows.

DON'T GO TO SLEEP ON THE JOB

In August 1841 the ballast between Bristol and Flax Bourton was being replaced with better-quality material. Had this work been carried out during the day, traffic would have been delayed, so it was done at night.

The gang executing this task temporarily stopped at 11.00 p.m. and waited until the mail had passed. During this break on 27 August, they all fell asleep – perhaps they had quenched their thirst with Somerset cider – and the head of an 'aged man', James Chorley, was across a rail. The mail approached without waking any of the sleeping men – they must have been in a very deep sleep not to have heard it or felt the vibrations. James' head was severed and his trunk divided just below the chest.

We in the twenty-first century must be much more sensitive than our nineteenth-century ancestors, as newspapers today would not reveal such gruesome detail.

CARING FOR ITS WORKFORCE

Some of the larger railway companies were very paternalistic. At Swindon the Great Western provided dwellings, schools, a hospital and a library.

The will of Francis Webb (1836–1906), Chief Mechanical Engineer of the London & North Western Railway, bequeathed money for the erection of a huge orphanage at Crewe. It had a 200ft-long frontage and provided accommodation for forty orphans of employees, twenty of each sex, with a large playground and various day rooms and sitting rooms.

The Mechanics' Institute at Swindon contained, among other things, a library and theatre.

THE CONDUCTOR ENTERTAINS

In August 2015 one South West Trains conductor brightened commuters' journeys between various stations between Surrey and Waterloo by holding quizzes over the public address system. Although mainly for peak-hour travellers, some passengers reported hearing the quizzes at off-peak times.

DOESN'T KNOW WHEN HE'S WELL OFF

On 19 July 1920 Robert Cowley, aged 54, an engine driver on the London & North Western Railway, was sentenced to twenty months' imprisonment with hard labour for stealing postal orders worth £2,545 17s 1d.

Employed by the LNWR since he was 13, he was considered one of the most reliable drivers and his wages averaged £6 5s 11d a week with the prospect of a pension. (Many railway workers at this time earned only half this sum.) His duty was driving the Travelling Post Office Euston–Crewe.

BARMOUTH BRIDGE

Barmouth Bridge has not been opened for over twenty years, a fact for which the local permanent way men are most grateful.

As the headway was low, it had to be opened for tall vessels to pass and this was a very time-consuming operation. Four permanent way men took out two pairs of a short length of running rail at each end of the bridge, then placed a key, which they had obtained from the Barmouth signalman, into a frame. The removal of this key from the signal box prevented the signalman inadvertently sending a train on to that section of the track and it plunging off the open bridge.

With the key inserted into the frame, this allowed two levers to release the locking bolts. The four men then turned handles to swing open the bridge and then close it again when the vessel had passed. If the day was hot, the bridge metal expanded and when they tried to close it they found that the bridge had grown slightly too long, jammed and needed small pieces of metal shaved off.

MAIL ROBBERY

In 1919 an engine driver and fireman employed on the South Eastern & Chatham Railway were charged with stealing six mail bags and contents between London and Faversham. During the Down journey the bags were thrown on to the line and on the Up trip they stopped the train and recovered them.

The fireman said that they burned the bags in the firebox and 'sorted out the stuff'. A Post Office clerk said the fireman had told him that he had cashed the postal orders and shared the proceeds with the driver. The driver claimed that he had received nothing, but knew what was being done, that the fireman had brought three bags each night, selected the letters he wanted and burned the remainder and the bags in the firebox. The driver said he had refused to accept anything from the fireman.

A RISKY JOB

It was far more dangerous being a railway employee than a passenger. Between 1841 and 1875, almost 6,200 employees were killed compared with 1,300 passengers. Between 1872 and 1875, almost 3,000 employees were killed, but safety features had reduced passenger fatalities to 155. In 1875, one in 334 employees was killed, but in 1899 only one in every 1,006.

HOW THE GWR ORGANISED A PARTY

FOR 20,000

How would you organise cake and tea for 20,000 guests? It was no problem for the GWR.

One of the great social events in Swindon was the annual children's fete held in the park, which was organised by the GWR. Each child received a ½lb slab of fruit cake and a free ticket for a roundabout ride. In 1891, 2 tons 16cwt of 5lb cakes were made.

Well before Henry Ford introduced the production line to his car factory, the principle was used at Swindon for cake cutting. The trimming shop foreman devised a cake-cutting machine with four cross-blades and one longitudinal blade in a press worked by a lever. The machine had a canvas belt feed that carried a cake to the cutter and then fed the sliced cake to tables, where ladies packaged it. This machine reduced the packing time to four hours.

Some 680 gallons of tea were brewed. The original idea was to empty chests of tea into locomotive tenders filled with cold water and then turn live steam from an engine into the mixture. The downside was that the resultant tea might have left something to be desired as a cheering beverage and if anyone had turned the wrong handle and started the injectors, the cones of the latter would have become blocked with tea leaves and result in another engine having to be ordered.

As E.L. Ahrons explains in *Locomotive & Train Working in the Latter Part of the Nineteenth Century*:

> The first thing to do was to have the tenders cleaned out. They were in a pretty bad state too, for the man who got inside to do the job came out in about ten seconds with the remark that if tea was to be made in those tanks he would turn over a new leaf and drink beer for the rest of his natural existence. However, they were finally got into a fair state of internal order, so that the resulting beverage in the end had only a moderate 'twang'.

Taps were fixed in the sides of the tenders and the hot water used to fill large tea urns, which were carried to the marquees for the guests to enjoy a refreshing drink.

THE NORTH BRITISH RAILWAY SAVES ITS
HOTEL GUESTS EMBARRASSMENT

When the North British Railway's hotel in Glasgow was reopened following rebuilding, it was discovered that the lavatory doors had no bolts. The problem was soon solved by sending out a member of staff to purchase 100 bolts and sockets at 10d each.

THE DANGERS OF STRIKE-BREAKING

The signal box at Portishead Junction, on the west side of Bristol, was set at the foot of a deep cutting with a sloping bank crowned by a low wall bordering the Bridgwater Road. Very early on Sunday, 20 August 1911, a disorderly rabble gathered there, at first jeering at the signalman on duty for breaking the strike. When they started to throw stones, he telegraphed to Temple Meads station for assistance.

In response, soldiers on duty at Pylle Hill were despatched by light engine. Temple Meads additionally contacted the Bridewell Police Station and a posse of constables set off for Portishead Junction in taxis and fire brigade vans.

Finding that the mob persisted in their attack on the signal box and the force for its protection was small, the military, under orders, fired blank cartridges over the heads of the mob. This steadied them for a time, but when the police arrived, they were forced to charge with batons.

This action proved effective and order was restored, but the police remained in the neighbourhood. The chief constable visited the scene and, on his instruction, one of the fire engines accompanied the police. The Bristol City Marine Ambulance was called out and an unconscious man suffering from concussion was taken to the general hospital in their wagon.

TAKE A HORSE TO WATER

For more than sixty years, a railwayman at Hatfield, Hertfordshire, had cleaned, polished and refilled a granite horse trough on the Great North Road near the entrance to Hatfield House, home to the Marquess of Salisbury. This was done under a 1910 agreement between the Great Northern Railway and Hatfield Parish Council. As no horse had used it for years, British Railways asked to be released from this agreement but the council refused.

THE LONG WAY ROUND

Most Metropolitan Railway trains ran clockwise round the Circle Line on the outer track, while the District Railway trains ran in the opposite direction on the inside line. At some stations both companies had ticket offices and some unscrupulous staff sold tickets for the longest route.

A HAT TRICK

In 1937, as a driver leaned out of his cab near Basingstoke, his cap blew off and sailed through the open window of a first-class carriage. It landed on the head of a passenger, who informed the guard imperiously that 'one does not pay a first class fare for this sort of thing to happen'.

At the next station the guard returned the cap to the driver and asked that in future he should make sure it went through a third-class window.

THE MYSTERY OF FOUR BRIDGES

Approaching Landore from the east, at Llansamlet cutting are what appear to be four useless bridges serving no apparent purpose. In actual fact, they are extremely useful structures.

When I.K. Brunel was building the South Wales Railway he found that the slopes of the cutting kept slipping. He used his ingenuity to design four flying arches, their tops heavily weighted with slag to counteract the enormous side pressure.

THE CLERGY PROVIDE LOCOMOTIVE
SUPERINTENDENTS

It was curious that in 1910 three of the largest railway companies had locomotive superintendents who were the sons of clergymen, and furthermore that they all came from East Anglia. They were: Henry Ivatt, Great Northern Railway; E. Earle Marsh, London, Brighton & South Coast Railway and Vincent L. Raven, North Eastern Railway.

Perhaps the solution to the curiosity was that given by Dr Temple speaking at Exeter Cathedral when he said that the further he travelled west, the more convinced he was that the Wise Men came from the east.

TYPO

'Yes,' said the grocer, as he paid the carriage on 3cwt of soap, 'the cost is exorbitant and I'm glad you have a man on the line who is honest enough to admit the fact.'

The expression on the face of the railway company's employee showed he was waiting for an explanation, so the shopkeeper continued: 'I read at the station this morning a notice about unclaimed goods on hand which stated "people to whom these packages are directed are requested to claim same and pay the awful charges on same" – and awful they are.'

The railway employee explained the printer had dropped the letter 'l' and the word was intended to be 'lawful'.

FALSE LIGHT

In 1913 an engine driver at Peterborough reported a light that appeared to be a green railway signal, but in actual fact was a mercury arc lamp outside a cinema. Similarly, an engine driver at Bath confused an illuminated sign on the roof of a corset factory with a railway signal. In the latter instance, a few tactful words with the management of the factory led them to place a shield so that it could not be seen from the railway.

Before green was made standard, a white light gave the 'all clear' to railway trains, but then there occurred many cases where the light of gas street lamps, particularly when fixed to an overbridge, caused a driver to believe erroneously that he had the right to proceed. The introduction of green signal lights obviated this difficulty.

OVERHEARD AT FINSBURY PARK STATION

Foreman porter: 'Why was Harrin gay'?

Assistant train destination shouter: 'Because Hornsey would grin.'

Then he continued with his work shouting: 'Harringay; Hornsey; Wood Green.'

ANOTHER MISSING DRIVER

In 1913 a London & South Western Railway engine driver was severely injured when he fell from his engine when travelling at 35mph just after it had passed through Dean station. Although a locomotive footplate is far from spacious, the fireman was so occupied that he did not miss him until the train was nearing Milford, Salisbury, some 8 miles further on.

TALLY HO

Early railway managers quickly grasped the remunerative value of carrying huntsmen – he travelled first class, took his horse, or horses, with him and usually a groom. He also made a return journey so there was no need for an empty stock movement to balance the service.

Some railways encouraged this traffic by offering special services: the London & North Western ran a slip coach between Euston and Leighton when required. Season hunting tickets were issued from 1 October until 30 April and sometimes special trains were run. For female hunters, the LNWR provided a special dressing room at Rugby station where they could change their clothes before and after a ride.

The Great Western Railway, in its timetables during the season, warned drivers to be on the lookout for hunts crossing the line.

Railways encouraged other sports: sometimes golfers had a halt opened to serve their links.

Sometimes help to a sport became a hindrance. Monkton Combe School near Bath wished to take an eight to a regatta at Saltford. Too long for one truck, the overhang was protected by a runner wagon. Unfortunately, the porter, in the interests of security, fixed the boat firmly to both wagons. You can guess what happened at the first curve!

FOG

Fog was particularly troublesome for railway working – modern electric colour light signals penetrate fog, but oil lamps were less successful. Signalmen had a 'fogging point' and when visibility prevented them from seeing this mark, they called out fogmen, who were usually permanent way men working overtime.

The railway provided them with a thick, warm coat, a hand lamp, a red and green flag and a supply of detonators.

On arrival at his signal, the fogman lit a fire in his 'red devil' and took shelter in his hut. He might be there for a night, or just an hour or two. Fogmen were visited periodically with hot tea or coffee and a couple of substantial beef sandwiches or similar fare. In due course he may have had to be relieved by a second turn man, then, after a rest, if the fog still persisted, may have been required to return for further duty.

When a signal was against a train, the fogman was required to lay a detonator on the track. When a train passed over, it would explode and indicate to the driver the position of the signal he was unable to see.

A detonator, about 2in in diameter, was made from tin and had two strips of lead fixed outside, 6in long and ½in wide, used to fasten the detonator to a rail. On the inside of the bottom of the detonator were studs with percussion caps fixed, the intermediate space filled with gunpowder, which was exploded by the engine wheels passing over the device.

If the fog was very thick it was not unknown for a fogman to have to climb a pole to see the position of a signal. On quadruple tracks it was sometimes necessary for him to cross a line to see the position of a signal arm and this could be highly dangerous in poor visibility. At some busy places, machines were used to place a detonator on a rail to avoid a fogman having to cross over.

WHAT THE WINDOW CLEANER SAW

The station master's house at Gosport formed the east end pavilion of the station. In front of it was the glass roof of the train shed, which became dirty, blocked some of the station master's light and so needed cleaning weekly.

Each Saturday morning the most junior porter was ordered to climb on the roof with a cloth and bucket of water and clean the glass thoroughly. In addition to the climbing and the dirt, there was often a wind that blew through him, so it was not a popular job, but then one day the porter became enthusiastic.

Two weeks earlier, the unpopular Mr Ford had left and been replaced by Mr Searle, who had a wife and children. All was revealed in more ways than one on the day the junior porter was sick and another lad told to clean the roof glass.

As he climbed up and settled himself on the apex, he glanced across and then realised why this job had become so popular. From his vantage point the cleaner could see right into the bedroom of the station master's teenage daughter. Eventually the station master learned the secret and changed the cleaning time to the afternoon.

PIGEON POST

One day an observant station master in the Welsh valleys noticed that two miners, travelling on season tickets, always brought a pigeon with them as they went to work, releasing it between the station and pit head. The station master, suspecting that some crime was being committed, borrowed a gun, shot the pigeon down and discovered two season tickets attached to its leg.

It transpired that four miners were working two by two on different shifts and sharing two season tickets. The first pair used them and then returned them by pigeon to the second pair, who used them to reach work. A second pigeon flew between the miners' homes and the colliery to provide tickets for the return journey.

DRIVERS EXPECTED TO BREAK A RULE

Automatic brake instruction 5 (f) stated that a driver must enter terminal and principal stations at a speed allowing him to stop using only the handbrake. Had this rule been enforced, traffic would have been delayed and congestion would have arisen because the use of the vacuum, or air brake, allowed a train to approach a station at a higher speed. The Board of Trade inspecting officers usually complained that rules were not kept, but supported the abolition of this one.

REASON FOR EQUAL PAY

In 1919, the National Union of Railwaymen Executive decided to oppose the employment of women at lower rates of pay then men, not out of chivalry to women railway workers, but for the selfish motive that if the railway companies had to pay men and women the same rates for the same work, they would prefer men and dismiss the women who had been taken on in wartime to replace men who had been conscripted.

A SCARED ENGINE DRIVER

On 4 November 1837 an accident occurred on the London & Birmingham Railway at an unidentified place known as 'The Galloping Ground' where drivers had a chance to open their regulators and reach a decent speed.

This particular driver had been drinking and his engine reached such a speed that he became frightened and applied the brake suddenly, causing the loose-coupled coaches to crash into its tender. Its centre coupling struck the locomotive an oblique blow sufficient to make the light four-wheeled engine derail, causing the death of one man. The locomotive was supplied by Edward Bury and the engine crews were under his control, not that of the railway company.

WHISTLE FOR YOUR DINNER

It was not unknown for railwaymen's homes to be close to a line. This gave footplate crews a wonderful opportunity of alerting their wives to when they were likely to arrive for a meal. Unlike most factory and office workers, footplate crews could not always book off at a stated time as, for example, a goods train could be delayed, or a crew asked to do overtime. As each driver sounded the locomotive's whistle in a way peculiar to him, wives were not confused by the signals of other drivers.

FIRE! FIRE!

At Bath the Great Western Railway had its own fire engine and on 18 June 1841 a fire broke out at Messrs Williams' brewery on Broad Quay. While the Sun Fire Insurance engine kept on the premises was immediately brought into operation, the GWR machine quickly arrived too, manned by GWR employees, and the flames were soon extinguished. At Swindon Works, a fire engine existed to well within living memory.

At Gosport one day an employee at Goodwillies' Timber Yard, which backed on to the railway, noticed a small fire and notified the Gosport Fire Brigade. Meanwhile, a locomotive was passing the timber yard, and the crew spotted the fire and offered to help. The offer was accepted and the fireman sprayed water from the footplate hose over the timber yard wall so successfully that when the fire brigade arrived they had almost a wasted journey.

MASKED GUARD

In the early days of railways, passenger guards had an elevated seat to keep an eye on the safety of the train and its passengers and also to enable them to exchange signals easily with the enginemen. A guard suffered dust thrown up as the ballast was often ashes or gravel, so to protect his eyes from this and the more serious damage from red hot coke from the locomotive firebox, some railways issued goggles.

THE EXPERIENCES OF A

PRISONER-OF-WAR

When the First World War broke out, John Aspinall, a locomotive engineer on the Lancashire & Yorkshire Railway, was in Hornburg. He left the spa on 17 August, but the Germans then sent him to a prisoner-of-war camp. Aspinall recorded:

> In order to obtain their food the prisoners in each building were lined up in fours and made to march down to the kitchen under an armed guard. They were admitted into the kitchen in twos, made to take their hats off, and served soup from a boiler: a soldier ladled the soup direct into bowls. They then passed on, and were formed into ranks four deep and had to wait until all had received their portion. The return to barracks was then made and food consumed. Sometimes the waits were very long, and prisoners were kept standing for one to one and a half hours, but this was a matter of organisation, and became better as the camp filled with prisoners.

On 9 September, he was moved to more comfortable quarters:

> Thirty-five of the senior and better educated men participated. They were taken to a higher part of the camp and put into a stone barrack called '12 M.B'. Here iron beds, used by soldiers, were supplied. They had straw mattresses. We were allowed certain privileges. For example we might now send one or two people for our food instead of having to march in ranks for it.

On 21 September Aspinall and a friend were sent for by the adjutant, who handed them their orders for release. He arrived in England on 24 September and the South Eastern & Chatham provided a special train to convey him from Folkestone to London.

A RAILWAY HERO

Porter Humphreys of Murton station on the North Eastern Railway performed a very plucky action after seeing a woman fall from the platform. He jumped down in front of an approaching train only 5yd away and held her in the 'four foot' while the engine and fish van passed over them before the train could be halted.

FREEBIES

Railwaymen tended to be poorly paid and took advantage of their work to obtain free gifts. Footplate crews, especially if working goods trains that had a more flexible timetable, could obtain bean sticks from the line side and carry them back on the engine. Mushrooms and watercress could be obtained in season. One driver on the Thornbury branch in Gloucestershire liked to stop and collect snails, which he cooked on the backplate of the firebox.

Householders whose gardens backed on to the railway could entice railwaymen to give them free coal. The trick was to paint a head – say of a cat – on a large piece of tin, cut a hole for a mouth and then wait.

The temptation was too great! Passing firemen would hurl a lump of coal at the target and try to score a goal through the mouth.

FISHY STORIES

The Stokes Bay Railway & Pier Company was formed to provide a short route to the Isle of Wight, and at Stokes Bay itself passengers could step easily from a train to the ferry. The engineer of this 1½-mile-long line was Hamilton Henry Fulton, whose greatest project was the Manchester Ship Canal. The Stokes Bay line opened on 6 April 1863. Although Queen Victoria herself never used this route, her luggage did, joining the Royal Train at Basingstoke.

As the pier station was actually sited over water, the imaginative staff cut a hole in the ticket office floor in order to drop a line through as the sea below the pier was a favourite location for various forms of flat fish.

In favourable weather, staff unofficially borrowed the boat that the railway was required to keep alongside the pier for life-saving and used it for fishing.

A resourceful signalman at Farleigh Down box, just east of Bath, whose cabin was close to a brook, made a 20ft-long rod to enable him to fish while on duty.

The box was heated by a coal range, the engineer's gang delivering 15cwt of coal annually, but with the box open continuously this proved insufficient. To renew the supply, the ploy was to wait for a light engine to come along, unhitch the signal wire so that it was inoperable, stop the light engine to give a written order to pass the signal at danger, invite the driver into the box to have a cup of tea while the order was written, and then suggest he may wish to ask his fireman to throw some coal from the tender. About 10cwt was usually decanted, the engine then proceeding on its way and the wire reconnected.

SOWING SEED

One gentleman, who travelled regularly on the Lynton & Barnstaple Railway in North Devon, threw flower seeds out of the window to beautify the track side.

Unfortunately his efforts did not prevent the number of passengers declining from 72,000 in 1925 to 32,000 in 1934. As expensive permanent way renewals were required, it was decided to close the line. A meeting was held at Barnstaple to try to reverse the decision, but the fact that all the railway's supporters had arrived from Lynton by car rather ruined their case.

The day following closure, the Barnstaple station master laid on the track a wreath sent by Paymaster Captain Woolf, R.N. (Retired) which bore a black-edged mourning card with the inscription: 'To Barnstaple and Lynton Railway, with regret and sorrow from a constant user and admirer; "Perchance it is not dead, but sleepeth".'

His wish is coming true: enthusiasts have relaid track at Woody Bay and hope eventually to relay the whole of this scenic line.

TRADE UNIONISTS OBJECT TO CLERGYMEN

In 1917 four clergymen assisted the war effort by qualifying as signalmen on the North Eastern Railway, but trade unionists objected to them entering railway service.

RAILWAYMEN OFFERED A VISIT TO THE
FIRST WORLD WAR BATTLEFRONT

It seems incredible, but according to the *Railway & Travel Monthly* of 1918 the British government issued an invitation to 400–500 railwaymen to visit the battlefront in order to obtain first-hand information on the war. Some men refused to go, believing that the effort made in arranging such trips should instead be put to winning the war.

BRUNEL'S OPINION

Brunel considered that education was likely to make a driver less careful and once stated that he preferred illiterate men, but certainly quite a few of his early drivers recruited from the North of England were literate.

On one occasion, instead of sending out printed instructions regarding new signals, he sent a special train down the line one Sunday to pick up drivers and firemen to take them to Paddington, where in two hours he explained the working and the meaning of the signals in various positions.

THE CONTRACT SYSTEM OF DRIVING

In the early days of railways some companies used the contract system of employing drivers. They were guaranteed their daily wage as a minimum and not allowed to work more than twelve hours daily. They were subject to a fine of 1s 0d per minute if they brought their trains in late at a destination, should the delay have been their fault. The contract driver had his coke, oil and other stores supplied at cost price and was paid from 3¾d to 4½d per train mile for passenger trains and 6d to 6½d for goods. The men were responsible for carrying out small repairs to their engine.

Using this system, the companies achieved a saving of 20 per cent on locomotive running costs and the men earned more than if they had been just paid for the time spent on duty. Fewer repairs were required because of the care drivers bestowed on an engine to keep it in good order.

A BUSMAN'S HOLIDAY

An interesting action was brought against the London & South Western Railway when a passenger sought to recover £15, the value of a bag stolen at Waterloo after it had been handed to a porter. The porter was actually employed at Hampton Court station and, after finishing his work there, had gone to Waterloo to do portering work for the sake of the tips.

The LSWR pleaded that it was not responsible, as the porter was working outside his scope of employment and the county court verdict was in favour of the railway company.

The plaintiff appealed to the divisional court and claimed that a passenger looking for a porter could not be expected to inquire if the porter was on or off duty, so this court reversed the decision and held that the passenger was entitled to recover the £15.

SHUNTER TO DRIVER COMMUNICATION

Towards the end of the First World War, an apparatus was in use that has received little publicity. At Southall West Junction, the Great Western Railway installed equipment that enabled a shunter to communicate with the driver. The transmitter's appearance was similar to a ship's telegraph dial and handle.

Three shoes on the engine picked up current from conductor rails, one laid alongside and the other between the running rails. Six instructions could be transmitted: Go ahead, Steady, Stop, Ease up, Back, and Back smart. Corresponding signals appeared on an illuminated indicator on the receiving instrument in the engine cab, a bell sounding in the cab the instant a signal was given. Three pick-up shoes were fitted on the engine, only two making contact at a time, the other coming into use when the engine was turned. The scheme was not adopted for general use as hand signals were almost as effective and cheaper.

A PLANNING OFFICE HELPS

FIRST WORLD WAR WOUNDED

The London & North Western Railway's Engineering Department was able to help wounded soldiers.

Linen was required for surgical dressings and other purposes in the war hospitals and the engineering department held thousands of unwanted plans and maps mounted on linen, so the paper was soaked off and, after washing at the LNWR laundry, was sent for use in the hospitals.

TRAPPED!

Electrification of the Southern Railway demanded new substations between Keymer and Newhaven. Probably to reduce costs, these were built by the Southern's own maintenance bricklayers. Work over, they were collected by special train to take them home to Brighton.

One Sunday afternoon the men were collected from Newhaven, Southease and Lewes, but when the engine whistled at Cooksbridge, nobody appeared. As the substation appeared to be finished, the footplate crew assumed that the bricklayers had gone home early, but when the workman's train arrived at Haywards Heath the foreman found he was fifteen men short. Standing on the platform was the company's General Manager, Sir Herbert Walker, together with the Chief Electrical Engineer and the Chief Electrical Engineer (New Works). Sir Herbert said: 'We must return to Cooksbridge.'

The engine, which had been watered, was run round the coach and ran smartly to Cooksbridge, where the three officials climbed out and walked to the substation.

There were no doors, but faint cries for help could be heard: the workers had bricked themselves in! The fireman was ordered to collect his coal hammer from the footplate and, taking it in turns, both electrical engineers hammered at the place where the entry door should have been. Their efforts resulted in only a small hole appearing in the brickwork.

Taking off his coat, Sir Herbert said: 'Let me try' and within a few moments had created a hole large enough for a man to crawl through. The first man out carried a drawing – it showed no doors.

5

TRACK

RAILWAY TO ROAD

The North Devon Link Road built on the erstwhile Devon & Somerset Railway between South Molton and Barnstaple, a distance of about 11 miles, is probably the longest length of former railway line to be replaced by a road.

PRESERVING SACRED TURF

When the Great Central Railway was extending its line to London, it needed to pass through the grounds of the Marylebone Cricket Club at Lord's.

Three parallel tunnels were required, but not actually beneath the turf where the matches took place. No disturbance was caused to the cricket season as the contractors took possession on 31 August 1896 and handed the ground back to the club on 8 May 1897. As the tunnels were to be only just below the surface, it was more expedient to use the 'cut and cover' method, rather than make a bore. Much of the original top soil was replaced together with sods taken from Morley's cricket ground at Neasden, which had been taken over by the Great Central.

The railway ingratiated itself with the cricket authorities by gaining permission to demolish an adjoining school, relocating it to Bushey and presenting the site of the former school to the MCC as extra land. The railway's entry into London also caused the homes of about 25,000 people to be demolished: some were rehoused and others displaced.

HOW WOULD NETWORK RAIL HAVE COPED

WITH BROAD-GAUGE CONVERSION?

Network Rail's slow progress with electrification leads one to ponder on how it would have dealt with the broad-gauge conversion in 1892.

The Great Western Railway had been built to the gauge of 7ft ¼in. Although an excellent idea as it offered greater stability and more space for more powerful locomotives and wider carriages, other railways had been built to the standard gauge of 4ft 8½in. Initially this did not matter, but as railways spread over the country, the difference in gauge prevented through running. This meant that goods needed to be transhipped from wagons of one gauge to another, with consequent expense and delay, while passengers were forced to change trains – particularly frustrating to Victorians with piles of luggage not of the carry-on case variety.

To avoid the problem, much of the GWR was given a third rail, set at the standard gauge, and this enabled the track to accommodate rolling stock of either gauge. The result was that by 1891 only the lines west of Exeter still remained broad gauge only. It was obvious that for economy the nettle would have to be grasped and all its tracks made standard gauge only.

During the weekend of 21–22 May 1892 the whole of the line between Exeter and Penzance, plus branches (a total of 177 miles) was converted in thirty hours. The work was carried out by about 5,000 men, working in gangs of twenty, with each gang converting

1½ miles of track. Could it have been done so efficiently and quickly today?

AN UNUSUAL LEVEL CROSSING

After the Second World War, the Bristol Aeroplane Company developed the large Brabazon airliner, which it hoped would carry vast numbers of passengers eager to explore the world after being confined to Britain during the hostilities. However, the BAC faced a difficult problem: if it built this large plane, the existing runway would be of insufficient length, while space for a new longer runway was on the far side of the GWR's Filton to Avonmouth branch.

The answer was an aircraft level crossing to offer a taxi-track from the building hangar to the new runway. When BAC wished to take an aircraft over this crossing, it rang Filton West signal

The Bristol Aeroplane Company's level crossing near North Filton Halt, 21 August 1980.

box and, if the line was clear, a release was given to the motors operating the sliding gates. Following the passage of an aircraft, BAC restored the gates to their normal position and, providing a proving circuit was made, normal train operation was resumed.

THE MYSTERY OF ANDERSON'S PIANO

In the summer of 1947 the author was driven in an uncle's Hillman Minx from Glasgow to Oban. In the Pass of Brander, the young lad was puzzled to see distant signals set at close intervals beside the Callander & Oban line. It was not until some years later that he read the solution to the mystery.

The pass was subject to falls of rock, so to minimise danger caused by derailment, speed was limited to 25mph during the day and 12mph at night. In order to speed the service, a 9ft-high fence was erected, with wires set 1ft apart. A falling rock would break at least one wire, causing a distant signal to show 'Danger'. This warning system permitted the speed restriction to be lifted. Wind caused the wires to hum, so it was nicknamed 'Anderson's Piano' after the company's secretary/manager.

DON'T TRY IT!

Would you be electrified if you urinated on the third rail? The answer is 'Yes', though if the stream was broken into drops and the gap between the drops was large enough, you would be insulated by the air.

THE FIRST SUSPENSION RAILWAY

Apart from the Barmen–Elberfeld Railway in Germany, the development of suspension railways has been confined to cableways used for mineral transport, but for passengers, suspension railways are now limited almost entirely to mountainous countries. However, this has not always been the case.

The first proposal for a suspended railway was made by Henry Robinson Palmer, engineer to the London Dock Company, who secured a patent for his system on 22 November 1821.

The first line to be built was in the Royal Victualling Yard, Deptford. Opened in the latter part of 1824, it transported stores from the bank of the River Thames to the warehouses.

In 1825, the year the Stockton & Darlington Railway opened, another Palmer line was erected at Cheshunt, Hertfordshire. This was to convey bricks and lime across the Cheshunt marshes to shipment on the River Lea.

Each wagon was suspended from a single rail from two cast-iron wheels with double flanges. A wagon had two compartments, one suspended on each side of the rail and each having a capacity of 20 cu ft. A train consisted of seven pairs of wagons, weighed 14 tons and was drawn by a horse.

Recycling being no twenty-first-century idea, the posts supporting the rail consisted of old oak ship's timber. In order to cope with the varying contours of the ground, to keep the line level the height of the posts varied from 2 to 5ft. The rail itself was formed of deal planks, 3in by 12in, placed edgeways in clefts in the posts. The upper surface of the rail was protected by an iron bar.

The opening ceremony took place on 25 June 1825, when the first wagon was converted to temporarily carry passengers. It was described in Volume II of the *Register of the Arts and Sciences* for 1825:

The vehicles glide so smoothly over the surface of the country, as to be compared only to the floating of boats in the stream of

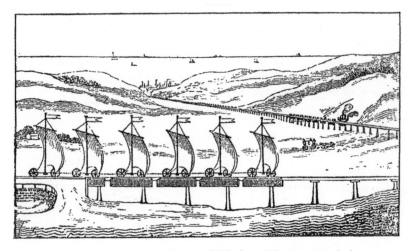

Luke Hebert's abortive scheme of 1824 for a Palmer suspended railway to transport fish between Brighton and London.

George Bennie's railplane at Milngavie.

a river; and it is evident that no mode of travelling can possibly be less free from danger. It possesses superior advantages to most situations, the friction must be full one third less than on other railways.

As early as 1824 Luke Hebert had proposed a Palmer railway to transport fish rapidly between Brighton and London using sail power. It is interesting to record that in 1826 Palmer exhibited a model railway at Elberfeld and a company was actually formed with the object of linking Barmen and Elberfeld with a line conveying coal, but it was three-quarters of a century later before these two towns were connected with the Langen suspended railway, which still survives.

A century after Palmer, his concept was developed and in 1929 the George Bennie railplane demonstration track was constructed between Milngavie and Hillfoot near Glasgow. The car, suspended by two-wheel bogies and stabilised by a lower rail, was moved by propellers fitted front and rear. The idea literally did not take off.

THE USEFUL TRAVERSER

A piece of equipment that has virtually disappeared due to the fact that locomotive-hauled passenger trains are now a rarity is the traverser. It came into its own where there was insufficient space for a crossover road to allow an engine to run round its train. Powered by steam, electricity, or worked manually, a traverser was simply a length of rail that moved an engine sideways to an adjacent track. Each traverser had three sets of running rails, thus ensuring that there was always rail at the end of a line and obviating the risk of a locomotive plunging into a pit.

A PNEUMATIC RAILWAY

Inventors have for a long time sought to improve on the traditional railway. The pneumatic railway at the Crystal Palace was an 1864 invention by T.W. Rammell. Placed in a 600yd-long tunnel, 10ft high and 9ft wide, the train was blown in one direction and sucked in the other.

A CHURCH BUILT FROM

RAILWAY SLEEPERS

The Church of St Walburge, just north of Preston station, is built from railway sleepers – no, it is not timber built, but of stone.

Many of the early railways used stone sleeper blocks as they were longer lasting than timber and offered a clear path between the rails, whereas timber sleepers were a trip hazard for horses. With the introduction of steam haulage and consequently faster travel, it was found that the less-rigid ride offered by timber sleepers was superior, so the stone blocks were replaced. The blocks were recycled, some for walls, and in 1867 the limestone sleeper blocks from the Preston & Longridge Railway were used to build the church.

A SUBSTITUTE CATCH-POINT

Usually a running line was protected from runaway wagons by a catch-point that would derail them, but the Associated Portland Cement Company, at Buriton, near Petersfield on the Portsmouth Direct line, used another method.

On one of the three sidings, instead of catch-points, a catch-hook was provided. This was lowered when the siding was being shunted, but was normally in the raised position. The *Western Appendix* to the *Southern Railway Working Time Table* explains:

> A length of chain is attached to the hook, and in the event of a wagon running away from the private siding towards the railway company's property, the axle of the wagon engages with the hook which is then released from a socket and the gradual running out of the chain attached retards the wagon until it is eventually brought to a stand.

BATS IN THE TUNNEL

As an economy measure, the double-track Oxford–Bletchley line was singled in October 1973, including the length through the 145yd Wolvercote Tunnel under north Oxford. The tunnel is occupied by bats and when Chiltern Railways wished to redouble the track, as double track brings trains closer to the tunnel walls, warning lights are switched on when a train approaches to give the bats a warning to fly off.

WHAT THE EYE DOESN'T SEE

In January 1856 the South Yorkshire, Doncaster & Goole Railway opened a branch to Thorne Waterside. When the Board of Trade inspector was about to arrive, it was realised that no loop had been provided to allow the engine to run round its train.

Quick thinking placed smartly dressed navvies in wagons attached to the inspector's train to give the appearance of shareholders. On arrival at Thorne, the inspector was taken to an inn for a drink and while he was out of sight, the navvies lifted the engine off the line, pushed the coach and wagons by and then re-railed the locomotive ready for the return journey when the inspector emerged from the hostelry.

WOODEN RAILS

In the 1840s William Prosser advocated substituting wooden rails for the expensive and unsatisfactory iron rails. In 1844 a mile of double-track 75lb/yd iron rails cost £3,000, whereas beechwood rails cost only £460, plus £70 for paynizing per mile. Labour for laying track on Prosser's system cost £100 a mile, compared with £150 for iron.

'Paynizing' was carried out by exhausting air from wood pores and forcing into them a solution of oxide of iron and lime, this semi-petrifying the wood and prevent rotting.

In 1843 a Bill was deposited to construct a line on Prosser's system between Woking and Guildford. Parliament sanctioned this Guildford Junction Railway, but then the London & South Western purchased the company in December 1844 and laid it with conventional iron rails.

An experimental short length of Prosser's track was put down and it was discovered that timber rails gave more 'bite', so a train

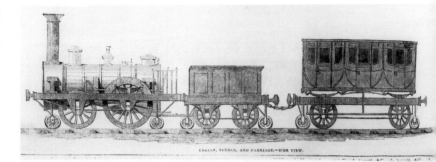

Prosser's experimental wooden railway on Wimbledon Common in 1845. The small wheels are set at an angle of 45 degrees to keep the larger wheels on track.

could ascend an incline of 1 in 9 even when the rails were wet, and a train moving at 24mph could stop in a distance of 24yd.

No flanges were placed on the wheels of locomotives or rolling stock, and they were kept on the rails by inclined guide wheels.

An experiment was carried out on the Hayle Railway, Cornwall. A loaded wagon, fitted with guide wheels and divested of flanges on its bearing wheels, could be propelled with a quarter less power than a similar wagon with flanges. As an inequality of track levels could lift the guide wheels from their positions and cause a derailment, vehicle frames were springless, but instead the bodies themselves were suspended on springs.

THE LONDON & NORTH WESTERN
RAILWAY'S MOUNTAIN LINE

The Pennines, as the backbone of England, formed a significant barrier to canals and normal railways, but as early as 1825 an Act was obtained to construct a railway over 30 miles long to link the Cromford Canal, 277ft above sea level, over a summit at Ladmanlow 1,266ft above sea level and down to Whaley Bridge on the Peak Forest Canal, 517ft above sea level.

The line, which was single track with passing loops, had a significant number of steep inclines, the most severe of which had necessarily to be worked by stationary steam engines. They were: Sheep Pasture Incline, 1,320yd at 1 in 8½; Middleton Incline, 1,100yd at 1 in 8½; Hopton Incline, 220yd at 1 in 14; and Whaley Bridge Incline, 178yd of 1 in 13½. In addition to the problems caused by the steep inclines, some of the curves were very tight, one having a radius of only 55yd. Two days could be spent transporting a load from one end of the line to the other and initially horses were used between the inclines.

Sixteen stationary steam engines were provided, two for each of the eight inclines. Initially hemp ropes were used, but these broke, and in 1856 were replaced by wire cables. It was a mineral line until 1855, when an Act was passed allowing the railway to carry passengers. The eight-hour journey was well patronised in the summer, but was withdrawn each winter when demand was low. From 1860, locomotives were used on stretches between inclines.

On 29 February 1888, Leap Year's Day, the rope broke, a raft of wagons derailed at the foot of Sheep Pasture Incline and leapt across both the Midland Railway and canal into a field beyond, not damaging the railway or canal. With the thought that perhaps next time they would not be so lucky, a catch pit was created to collect any such runaways.

Points were fitted at the entrance to the pit and the pointsman in charge closed the points when he was satisfied that the descending wagons were under control; if they were not, he left the points open so they would be diverted safely into the pit. At night, a red light was carried on the first wagon of a run – contrary to the usual practice of showing a white light at the front of a train. To help the pointsman judge the speed of a rake of wagons, a treadle-operated gong sounded in his cabin and the intervals between the gongs enabled him to judge the speed.

As the Hopton Incline was only 220yd long it could be 'rushed' by a locomotive, but in unfavourable weather, platelayers spread sand on the rails, and if this did not give the wheels sufficient grip a train would be divided and taken up in two portions.

When the line was first worked by locomotives, a special type was employed with a rope-winding drum like a ploughing engine. A locomotive first climbed an incline alone and would then haul up the wagons. As water was a problem at some of the higher levels, it was conveyed in tank wagons to supply stationary engines, locomotives and railwaymen's cottages.

A FISHY STORY

In the December 1914 edition of the *Railway & Travel Monthly* a correspondent wrote:

> I was surprised the other day, when working on the Midland Railway, near one of the locomotive water troughs at Melton, to see a school of minnows, numbering from 50 to 80, swimming about in the trough. I wondered how long they would escape the scooper of the engine, and what would happen to the feed pipes of the engine if they were not fortunate enough to escape.
>
> My fears were soon set at rest by a remarkable strategy on the part of the fishes. The troughs were something like 400 yards long, and are refilled from a 10-inch pipe in the middle of the trough. Immediately on the approach of an engine at the far end of the trough, the fishes swam to the drain, from which I may say they never get very far, and there waited until the engine had passed over, and as soon as they felt the inrush of a fresh supply of water, they swam out and waited about until they had to shelter again.
>
> I noticed the operation take place for three trains, and was amazed at this example of sagacity. I may say that the water in the tanks is taken from a river nearby, which accounts for the presence of the fishes.

The editor commented: 'Possibly the drain was at the far end of the trough. If so, the minnows would naturally swim as far away as possible from an approaching train; and would do so each time they heard a noise. If such be the case, the "sagacity" is nothing to be amazed at.'

PUMPING ENGINE

On the evening of 9 May 1915 a terrific storm caused the Fleet sewer to flood the Metropolitan Railway's widened lines between

King's Cross and Farringdon Street stations, causing the passenger service to be suspended. As the Metropolitan had previously experienced similar trouble here, to cope with a reoccurrence the company's engineers had constructed a pump that could be attached to the front buffer beam of any of their locomotives. It was capable of raising 700 gallons of water per minute.

BRUNEL'S INGENUITY TO PREVENT

A TRAIN RUNNING AWAY

When the Great Western Railway proposed placing Box Tunnel on a gradient of 1 in 100, Dr Dionysius Lardner claimed that if the brakes failed on this slope, a train would emerge at 120mph. Brunel showed that the doctor had overlooked both friction and air resistance from his calculations, and that these would reduce the speed to 56mph.

Nevertheless, Brunel believed it prudent to reassure nervous passengers by replacing the bridge rails that he favoured, shaped like an inverted 'U', with rails designed to slow a train. On the Down line through the tunnel he used two flat iron plates 7in wide and ¾in thick, laid on a layer of compressible felt and inclined slightly inwards. This design caused the weight of the train to bend the rails down and thus cause retardation as it had to proceed on an undulating surface. It was so effective that it took nine minutes to pass through the tunnel at a speed of 11mph.

It also caused a problem, because for a few weeks following its opening, only the Down line was completed and consequently Up trains also had to use it. The braking effect of the special rails, combined with the steep gradient, frequently meant that even with the assistance of a banking engine Up trains took half an hour to pass through.

The special retarding track was proved an unnecessary precaution and in June 1851 the Down line through the tunnel was laid entirely with conventional track.

LNWR ON THE LSWR

The Wool–Bovington Camp Railway in Dorset was constructed during the First World War to give access to a tank repair depot. Although connecting with the London & South Western Railway at Wool, it had the appearance of a London & North Western Railway branch, with LNWR-type gradient and notice boards, mile posts etc. This was accounted for by the fact that the engineer in charge of its construction was Captain A. R. Finlayson, Royal Engineers, formerly of the LNWR Engineer's Department.

The branch, 2½ miles in length, had two sidings at the camp, each long enough to hold twenty-four Rectanks – special vehicles for carrying army tanks. The name, reminiscent of the Great Western Railway's telegraphic code words used for identifying their stock, came about quite differently. 'Tank' came from the load they were designed to carry, and as the War Department required the Railway Executive Committee to have a suitable wagon on which tanks could be loaded and unloaded, the 'REC' comes from its initials.

The majority of Rectanks were constructed by the LNWR. These bogie wagons weighed about 15½ tons and, as the large tanks weighed 35 tons, a full train of twelve tanks amounted to about 600 tons plus the brake van. The exceptionally low platform of a Rectank, only 3ft 6½in above the rails, kept the load within the loading gauge.

As tanks were driven over the ends of wagons when being loaded, or offloaded, screw jacks were placed below the sole bars to support their weight. After loading, tanks were scotched, chained and sheeted. The Rectanks and their load crossed the Channel by train ferry via either Richborough or Southampton.

TENDER-FIRST

An engine crew was not anxious to work an engine tender-first if this could be avoided. Unless the day was hot, cold air was scooped into the cab, making conditions highly unpleasant. One crew known to the author worked tender-first on the outward trip when they were going slowly, and then chimney-first on the home trip when they were proceeding at a faster pace.

Tank engines were favoured for use on lines where it was not possible to turn an engine, because a tank engine has a back to offer shelter. Banking engines have to spend half their lives running in reverse and to make life rather more pleasant, some had tender-cabs fitted.

One banking engine not fitted with a tender-cab became derailed while travelling back downhill tender-first. The ensuing

Somerset & Dorset Railway 2-8-0 No. 80 at Derby in photographic grey livery, 1914. Initially the turntable at Bath was too short to turn it, so half of its mileage was travelling backwards. To make this more pleasant for the crew, a tender-cab was fitted.

investigation revealed that the crew had not been on the footplate but were sheltering from the bitter wind standing on the buffer beam in front of the smokebox and so had not observed the snowdrift.

As little steam was required for the descent, the fireman was not needed in the cab, and the driver controlled the locomotive's speed by the unorthodox method of opening the end of the brake pipe with a stout knife, admitting air and triggering the automatic brake.

A POINT FOR NARROW- (STANDARD-)

GAUGE TRAINS ONLY

At Bathampton, the Up road was mixed gauge and that leading off to Bradford-on-Avon narrow (standard) gauge. So that the road was never wrong for an Up broad-gauge train, Brunel arranged that no movable point blade was necessary. A check-rail on the inside narrow-gauge curve drew the other wheels away from the outer broad-gauge rail while they were running on their flanges for about 9ft. Although this was certainly safe for broad-gauge trains, it proved a danger to one on the narrow gauge.

On 11 June 1875, the 10.01 a.m. Bristol–Salisbury passenger train, consisting of six coaches and a guard's van hauled by Metro class 2-4-0T No. 970 built in September 1874, failed to take the points at the junction, causing the locomotive, van and two leading coaches to overturn. One frightened passenger jumped out and was killed when a coach fell on him. Another passenger was fatally injured. The *Bath Chronicle* reported that two men 'with much foresight took with them to the scene of the accident brandy and other stimulants which were found very useful'.

The inquest certainly had its lighter moments. Thomas Baker, an upholsterer, said: 'When the train came to a stoppage, I looked out and seeing the carriage before me thrown over, I thought it was time to get out (A laugh).'

Another passenger, John Hutton, recounted:

> When we entered the station I became alarmed at the rate we were going. Four of us were talking, and we saw we were going too fast and laid hold of the seat, knowing that at the rate we were going, the train could not take the points for the branch line. We were travelling at the same rate as the through trains on the main line. I listened to hear whether the engine would take the points and heard the engine strike. I cried out, 'She's off the line, I thought it would come to this.' I was in the carriage next to the van, it toppled about and then fell over, and I became insensible. When I came to myself I found my right leg out of the window dragging along and the train going on. When it stopped I got out of the carriage by climbing out of my window.

The coroner queried: 'I don't exactly understand how your leg could be hanging out of the window.' Witness: 'It was dragging on the ground. I cried out, "Oh, I shall lose my leg," and then put my hand out and pulled it in (Laughter).'

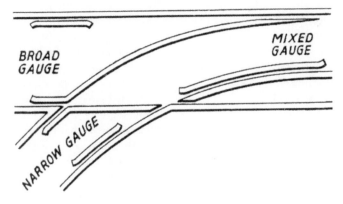

A mixed-gauge turnout using no movable point blade. Check rails pull wheels on to the correct track.

At the inquest it was believed that the figures in the signalman's register may have been altered. W. Lewis, a Bath photographer, made a copy, enlarged it ten times and it was then seen that the record had not been falsified. This was one of the first instances of photography being used for such a purpose.

The Board of Trade officer, Colonel Yolland, reviewing the accident, believed it had been caused by the train passing the junction at about 27mph and recommended a maximum of 10mph. He also urged that double movable switches be installed for both broad- and narrow-gauge lines, and that a length of broad-gauge rail be laid on the branch to provide for possible overrunning of an Up broad-gauge train against signals. He observed that similar junctions at Thingley and Calne Junction also needed similar improvement.

DON'T FORGET THE EIGHT-NINTHS YARD

OF PERMANENT WAY

We generally look to Scotsmen for minute financial accuracy, but the Isle of Man report for 1916 does not take second place in comparison with any from Caledonia.

'There have been relaid, with heavier section of steel rails and improved fastenings, 1 mile 243 8/9ths yards of main-line during the past year.'

The fact that 4in of line were necessary to complete a further yard was surely not required in an annual report, besides, when was the measurement made? A difference of a few degrees in the temperature when measuring would have resulted in more than the 8/9ths of a yard in the total given.

THE HUNDRED OF MANHOOD

& SELSEY TRAMWAY

The Hundred of Manhood & Selsey Tramway – for brevity it was generally known as the Selsey Tramway – was a line with a curious name. 'Hundred', in addition to the number, also means a sub-division of a county. The line ran from Chichester to Selsey Bill. Selsey was a small fishing village that at the end of the nineteenth century was becoming a tiny seaside resort.

The light railway, or tramway, was the first to be constructed after the passing of the Light Railways Act of 1896 and proved very useful for villages that had hitherto been up to 9 miles from a railway station.

The line started from Chichester alongside the London, Brighton & South Coast Railway, where it made a junction, and ran for about 8 miles to Selsey; there were four intermediate stations and two halts. A drawbridge spanned the Chichester & Birdham Canal. As the land was flat, almost no earthworks were required and all roads were crossed on the level except for an overbridge that carried a road over a cutting at Selsey. A train was required to approach an ungated crossing slowly, whistle a warning and be prepared to stop. Another economy was having no signals. Ballast was obtained free from a cutting near Selsey.

The railway had three locomotives, seven carriages, a luggage van and twenty-five goods vehicles. Two of the engines were purchased new from Avonside, Bristol. The other was a 3ft 6in-gauge 0-4-0ST ex-East Cornwall Railway that had been converted to standard gauge and a pony truck added, making it a 0-4-2ST. The three four-wheel coaches came from the Lambourn Valley Railway in 1910 when it was bought by the GWR. The remaining four were bogie vehicles.

Waiting rooms at the stations were of corrugated iron painted white, and each station had a short siding. To enable the concern to be run economically without having to pay booking clerks, tickets were sold on the train. First-class passengers were known

A Shefflex railcar passes an ungated level crossing north of Ferry station on the Hundred of Manhood & Selsey Tramway. Note the roof rack for luggage.

as 'saloon passengers'. Hunston and Selsey were the only staffed stations and Selsey and Chichester the only ones with gas lamps. The company offices and engine shed were at Selsey.

The chief engineering work was a drawbridge over the canal at Hunston, kindly paid for by the Chichester Corporation and rented to the tramway for a very reasonable £2 per annum. The line opened on 27 August 1897 only as far as a platform later known as Selsey Bridge, the bridge itself being incomplete. At the ceremony the Mayor of Chichester remarked that he was delighted that people could now go to the seaside at Selsey instead of Bognor, whose inhabitants had always been rather 'stand-offish'.

Initially the railway company did not commit itself to arrival times, and in the words of a visitor who travelled on the line a year later, 'I am rather surprised that they do so now. It is an over-bold stroke of policy.' The same visitor went on to describe the provision of the locomotive water supply at Hunston:

Imagine, O reader, an elevated platform supported by four rough timber piles, and a small cistern with a pump thereon, the latter being assiduously worked by a small boy in his shirt sleeves, whistling and happy. A pipe led down into a little stream trickling in a ditch by the side of the road from which the small boy pumped up the water with all his might.

The track soon became so overgrown with grass and weeds, in some places 2–3ft high, that the rails were almost invisible.

The company changed its name in 1924 to the West Sussex Railway, which flowed more sweetly off the tongue. That year, due to the increased road traffic, the ungated crossings were proving dangerous, so the Ministry of Transport insisted that trains must stop for the fireman or guard to advance into the middle of the road armed with a red flag by day, or red lamp at night.

Although cars and motor buses robbed the line of some passengers, there was significant agricultural traffic augmented by lobsters and crabs from Selsey. Economies were made by working most trains with two-car, petrol-engined railbuses: a Ford of 1923 and a Shefflex of 1928. They were actually ordinary road buses fitted with railway wheels and generally coupled back-to-back, sometimes separated by a luggage wagon.

R.W. Rush wrote in the *Railway Magazine* for April 1935 of a trip in the Shefflex: 'The roar of the engine, the exhaust fumes, the bumping and swaying as the car passed over the uneven track, all combined to impress the journey on the memory. The villagers, however, seemed inured to it.'

The locomotive shed at Selsey, built of timber, was capable of holding six engines. It resembled a garage, particularly as it had a petrol pump outside for the railcars. Despite economies, the railway became bankrupt in 1931 and closed on 19 January 1935.

A GOOD IDEA IF IT WORKED

In 1841 most sleepers were semicircular in section, a tree trunk being cut through the centre, the flat portion laid on the ballast and chairs fixed to the rounded part.

On the South Eastern Railway, triangular sleepers were cut diagonally from a square baulk. Chairs were fixed to the flat section, the pointed side being placed downwards, the idea being that the weight of trains would force the sleeper into the ballast and thus secure the track. Experience showed that this was not so: it only wobbled about instead of forming a firm foundation.

THE ORIGIN OF BALLAST

Collier brigs carried coal from ports in north-east England to London and for want of cargo, had to return weighted with Thames ballast in their holds. Thus enormous quantities of stone were formed in Shields and other ports, so when railway construction started in the north this provided a useful source of stone for bedding the track.

RUNAWAY ENGINE AT DONCASTER

The uninitiated believe that driving a steam engine is a simple matter – just opening the regulator, or moving the brake handle – but all railways, including today's preserved ones, insist rightly on a long course of training before a person is placed in charge of a locomotive.

A Great Northern Railway fireman who had only five weeks of experience as a cleaner and two weeks as a fireman was told by his driver, who was leaving the footplate, to move the engine. He had no driving experience and, loath to admit it, remained silent.

When the signal dropped, he blew off the brakes with the large ejector, leaving it in the 'Full off' position, and partly opened the regulator. Before reaching the signal box, he tried to stop the engine by pulling down the large ejector handle to completely destroy the vacuum. He had not opened the small ejector (which he probably knew nothing about), and failed to close the regulator. The engine continued to run against the brake, whose power diminished due to the lack of any ejector maintaining the vacuum and collided with a standing train.

6

ACCIDENTS

PASSENGER UNAWARE THAT HER TRAIN

HAD BEEN IN AN ACCIDENT

The broad gauge was inherently safe, due to the greater stability of its rolling stock, and what would have been a disaster on the standard gauge proved only fatal to the footplate crew of a broad-gauge train.

On 8 September 1852, the 9.45 a.m. express from Paddington was drawn onwards from Bristol by Bristol & Exeter 4-2-2 No. 20. The train consisted of an iron-built luggage van, and two first- and two second-class coaches. No. 20 approached Creech aqueduct between Bridgwater and Taunton at 44mph. Immediately beyond, the locomotive derailed and headed into the embankment, its tender somersaulting and landing upside down on the boiler.

Fortunately, the coupling behind the van broke, thus allowing the coaches to freewheel past the derailment. So little were the passengers disturbed that one lady said that she saw an engine pass rapidly in a contrary direction and only afterwards realised it was the derailed locomotive of her train.

TAR HALTS A TRAIN

On the first Saturday of the summer timetable for 1950, at about 12.25 a.m., Porter Sell at Christchurch station, following the passing of the Hamworthy–Eastleigh goods, detected a whiff of what he believed to be creosote.

He advised the signalman, who arranged for the train to be stopped and examined at Brockenhurst. In the darkness all seemed to be in order so the train proceeded to Bevois Park, Southampton. There, someone spotted the end of a wagon splashed with tar, and that the tank wagon in front of it had both its outlet and contents missing.

Dawn revealed that the outlet valve had become detached just after crossing the bridge over the River Stour just west of Christchurch and about 3,000 gallons of tar had escaped on the climb through Hinton Admiral. By the time it reached Sway, the tank was completely empty.

The 3.25 a.m. Up freight from Bournemouth was unaffected, but the rising sun melted the tar, causing the 5.38 a.m. Poole–Southampton passenger train to stall on the gradient of as steep as 1 in 103 through Hinton Admiral and seven more trains were affected before a light engine applied sand to counter the lubricant.

Bulleid's Pacifics were prone to slip at the best of times and the tar intensified the problem. Their sandboxes emptied quickly and their firemen stepped down on the track, throwing ballast under the driving wheels in an effort to obtain a grip.

The train most affected was the 7.20 a.m. Bournemouth West–Waterloo, which had to commandeer an engine from a Down freight to assist it to Brockenhurst. It lost forty-one minutes, while the total time lost by the eight trains was 155 minutes.

TROUBLED WITH THE WIND

An unusual accident occurred at the end of September 1875 on the Garstang & Knott End Railway. A high wind set two carriages in motion at Pilling and blew them along for 3 miles, damaging the leading coach and also the level crossing gates through which it passed.

AN UNRECORDED ACCIDENT

The local paper had a new reporter who was making a final round for news. Seeing the station master, he said: 'I understand there was an accident on your line last night.' The station master replied: 'Indeed, and which train met with an accident?' 'Why the one due here at 7.45,' said the news hound. 'That train, sir, arrived here punctually.' 'Yes, that was the accident I referred to.'

THE FIREMAN'S FINGER

A novel claim for compensation was brought successfully against the Great Western Railway at Uxbridge County Court in 1912. A fireman had cut one of his fingers while eating his dinner at his lodging. Blood poisoning set in and the finger eventually had to be amputated.

Naturally enough, the GWR appealed against the decision and, without even hearing the railway's side of the case, the judge of the Court of Appeal reversed the decision of the county court judge, being of the opinion that there was no evidence to justify the finding that the accident 'arose out of, and in the course of, the man's employment'.

A LUCKY ESCAPE

On 24 January 1914 the 3.50 p.m. Up express from Brighton was running at 70mph north of Balcombe Tunnel. Then 4-4-2T No. 25's connecting rod broke at the little end, the rod whirling round the crank axle and disabling the brake gear, so that the train ran ¾ mile before Driver Fred Smith could bring it to a halt. The right-hand cylinder, piston rod and guide were broken, the ashpan ruined and a dent made in the boiler. It was fortunate to come off so lightly, as the South Eastern & Chatham had experienced a similar breakage a few days before that resulted in its No. 172 being lifted up and derailed.

OFF & OVER

In 1915 the 8.40 a.m. express from Inverness to Perth comprised four composite coaches, four fish vans, an empty luggage van and a guard's van. Just after leaving Blair Atholl, one of the fish vans derailed on the points at South Blair Atholl. The event was unnoticed and the derailed wagon continued bumping over the sleepers for 3½ miles to Killiecrankie where the single line became double to make a passing loop. The van passed through the station at 40mph, but at the south end the derailed van swerved right round, its wheels torn off. It fell on its side across the line and the rest of the train stopped safely on a viaduct beyond the tunnel.

WIND CAUSES A RAILWAY ACCIDENT

On 20 September 1850 a cheap excursion train originating from Bath was returning from Paddington. As was the custom, it stopped at Swindon for a change of locomotive and *Ajax*, a 0-6-0 goods engine, was placed at the head of the train. At about

11.30 p.m., just beyond Wootton Bassett station and running at 25–30mph, the passengers felt a tremendous concussion. Their train had collided with a horsebox that a south-easterly wind had blown down a gradient of 1 in 660.

The engine and the first four carriages were precipitated down the embankment into a field of mangold-wurzels. The first carriage was turned on its side and its roof had to be broken with a sledgehammer to release the occupants. 'The screams of the female passengers was heart-rending.' Fortunately, the coupling chain behind the fourth coach snapped, so the remainder of the train did not fall on the wrecked coaches and cause loss of life.

William White, the policeman (a forerunner of a signalman) on duty at Wootton Bassett, was immediately placed in custody. The case was heard before the county magistrate. White had been verbally advised by Skull, the day policeman, that the horsebox was secure, but White had not personally checked that it was correctly scotched with triangular pieces of wood on both sides of the wheels. A public footpath crossed the line by the horsebox and a person could have removed the scotches. Nevertheless, White was found guilty of neglect and imprisoned for two months.

A SERIOUS LANDSLIP

Tracks beside the sea, although delightful for passengers, cause problems to engineers, the stretch of line at Dawlish being just one example.

Another was that at Folkestone Warren between Folkestone and Dover, though it was the strata rather than the sea that caused the problem on 19 December 1915.

About 6.30 p.m. a watchman near the east end of Martello Tunnel heard a rumbling sound. Knowing that an Ashford–Dover train was imminent, he summoned help from soldiers at a sentry post near the beach. They secured red flags round oil lamps and walked along the sinking railway towards the tunnel.

The driver of the 4-4-0 hauling four bogie coaches observed the warning lights before he emerged from the tunnel, but was outside before it stopped. The 130 passengers felt their carriages creaking and moving as the soft chalk advanced over the blue clay. The passengers climbed out and were led back through the 532yd-long tunnel to Folkestone Junction.

The following morning it was a bizarre scene as, although the train was mostly on the track, it resembled a dip in a fairground roller coaster. The permanent way was far from permanent, as it was buried to a depth of several yards for a distance of about 1,000ft, and at one point the line had been thrust seawards for 160ft.

Other railwaymen on the line enjoyed an equally lucky escape. The signalman at Abbots Cliff had been alerted by a platelayer, who warned him to stop all trains. Minutes later, he returned to advise him to leave his box as the cliff was moving. As the two men made their escape, the hillside collapsed and the signal box was swept away. The damage was so severe that the line remained closed for the rest of the First World War and only reopened on 11 August 1919.

REPAIRING A SHOVEL ON A RAIL

A London & South Western Railway driver was killed at Basingstoke when repairing a shovel on one of the rails of a line linking the engine shed with the running lines. The county court judge came to the conclusion that to get off his engine and trim a shovel on the running rail was not a thing he was employed to do and therefore his family should receive no compensation.

A BOY AGED 9 AND HIS MOTHER SAVE

A RUNAWAY TRAIN

In the early days of the Birmingham & Gloucester Railway, several wagons were left at the top of the Lickey Incline and started to roll down. A 9-year-old lad, seeing the danger, jumped on one wagon and applied the brake. It had insufficient power to stop the train but, instead of jumping off, he called to his mother, who jumped on another wagon and applied its brake, bringing the runaway train to a stand.

A RUNAWAY TRAIN

An unusual railway disaster involved a troop train on 15 September 1917.

A party of Royal Scottish Fusiliers were paraded at the Catterick Camp station to entrain for Edinburgh. The train, minus engine, was standing at the platform and the soldiers started to board. The carriages then started to run down the incline and after about 3 miles came to a sharp curve. Nine derailed, some smashed and others overturned, killing three soldiers and injuring forty to fifty. The leading carriage became uncoupled from the rest and, keeping to the rails, ran on to the next station, where it demolished the buffer stops and ended on the ballast. Had the engine been attached before the men boarded, the accident would not have occurred.

TRAIN CRASHES INTO THE

LOCOMOTIVES HAULING IT

On 16 November 1922 a Glasgow & South Western Railway goods train left Girvan headed by two locomotives. After passing Pinmore, 5 miles south of Girvan, the coupling between the tender of the second engine and the first wagon snapped but the two locomotives continued, unaware that there was anything amiss. There was a falling gradient of 1 in 70 at this place and the wagons gathering speed, eventually crashing into the tender of the second engine and causing twenty-one wagons to be derailed and a number of cattle to be killed. The footplate crews were uninjured.

7

ROLLING STOCK

LOO LAWS PROBLEM

From January 2020 the Persons With Reduced Mobility Regulations required all train lavatories to comply and be wheelchair accessible. The cost of modifying Class 150 Pacers was so great that the Welsh government decided not to do so. As there is no rule stating that a train must have a lavatory, it solved the problem by locking all the lavatory doors.

NO CHARGE FOR SPENDING A PENNY

In December 2016 Network Rail decided to abolish the 50p charge to use its toilets at Victoria, London Bridge and Charing Cross stations. The charge had earned Network Rail £6.4 million over nine years at Victoria alone. Between 2007 and 2016, Network Railway had earned more than £37.5 million from passengers paying 50p, 40p or 30p at the twelve stations it owned.

CARING FOR THE DISABLED

Caring for the disabled is not a new phenomenon; early in the twentieth century, most of the major railway companies provided special carriages for them. The Great Northern Railway constructed a multi-purpose vehicle at Doncaster that could be used either as a family parlour or an 'invalid saloon'. Electrically lit and steam-heated, it had large windows to offer extensive views of the countryside.

The family/invalid compartment was placed in the centre of the vehicle to offer easy riding, with 4ft-wide double doors and a floor covered by felt and a Wilson carpet. A toilet compartment adjoined and a luggage compartment was provided, while additional day/night compartments catered for attendants or servants.

The other major companies had similar saloons. The Great Western Railway, usually differing from other companies, had a couch on suspension slings, thus offering freedom from vibration. To secure the use of an invalid coach, generally four first- and four third-class tickets had to be purchased.

The South Eastern & Chatham, London Brighton & South Coast and the Great Eastern, in addition owned an invalid 'Road & Rail' coach, to enable a sick person to travel from home to home without change of coach. The rubber-tyred coach was drawn by horse to a station, where it was placed on a carriage truck and then at the destination station it again proceeded by road. Inside the coach was a suspended couch and if required this could be taken from the road coach to the invalid compartment of the train coach.

PIGEON POST

A very important traffic on the railways until about fifty years ago was the cartage of carrier or homing pigeons. The London & North Western Railway was the first to provide special vans for this traffic, these entering service in April 1906. The six-wheeled vans had racks on their walls and each van could carry thirty-six baskets. Gangways were provided at each end of the van to enable attendants to walk the length of a pigeon special.

On 7 July 1911 a special train containing 4,840 racing pigeons in 387 baskets left Huddersfield for Southampton, where the train stopped by a hydrant so that the birds could be watered. They were then placed on a railway steamer, carried to St Malo and then went on by French train to be released at Rennes.

THE CANNY SCOTS

Initially when toilets were fitted in carriages, rather than being accessed along a corridor, the door led straight from a compartment, with the result that one seat was lost. The Caledonian Railway overcame this problem by fixing a seat to the lavatory door – but if you wished to use the toilet and a person of the opposite sex was sitting on that seat, it could cause embarrassment to a sensitive soul.

PROVED WRONG

When steam locomotives were withdrawn from the underground sections of its line, the Metropolitan Railway painted the upper parts of its coaches cream, expecting that the sulphuretted hydrogen being absent, the colour would retain its smart appearance. This proved a fallacy and it reverted to an all-teak base with gold lining and a coloured crest.

RAINBOW LIVERY

In October 1903 the coaches of the Ealing & South Harrow Railway had novel liveries: the two trains of four cars, each having the first coach painted a greenish colour, the second and third with white upper panels and red lower, and the fourth a greenish-yellow like the first. A third train was composed of one car with white upper and red lower panels, and three cars a bright red.

COMMUTER LUXURY

On 1 June 1910 the Metropolitan Railway began running Pullman cars on its underground line. Originating at both Aylesbury and Chesham, they served various stations between Baker Street and Aldgate. They allowed businessmen to have an extra half an hour in bed and eat breakfast in the Pullman car. Golfers could catch the afternoon Saturday train from the City and lunch en route to the links. Theatre-goers could catch the 11.35 p.m. Down and eat dinner on the train.

The Pullman cars had to be specially designed to fit the Metropolitan loading gauge but were painted in the standard Pullman colours of umber and white.

The first Up car was on the 8.30 a.m. from Aylesbury, reaching Aldgate at 9.59; the next the 8.55 a.m. from Chesham for Liverpool Street. On Mondays to Fridays there was the 1.35 p.m. from Aylesbury to Baker Street and the 4.15 p.m. to Aldgate; and the 9.15 p.m. from Verney Junction to Baker Street.

Down trains comprised the 10.07 a.m. from Aldgate; the 12.05 p.m. from Baker Street; the 5.22 p.m. from Aldgate; the 6.08 p.m. through to Verney Junction and the theatre train leaving Baker Street at 11.35 p.m.

HOPPERS' SPECIALS

In the summer of 1912 the coaches set aside for hop pickers' specials on the South Eastern & Chatham Railway were block trains of small four-wheeled coaches withdrawn two or three years earlier after working mid-Kent services. Special trains were essential as the hoppers were rough, dirty and smelly, and after such use other passengers would have found them offensive, so for these trains it was only profitable to use coaches withdrawn from service and awaiting scrappers' ministrations.

In 1912 the return of hoppers from Kent to London took place on 21–29 September and inconvenienced businessmen residing in the Surrey outer-suburban district of the SECR.

Many of these evening services started from London Bridge Low Level station and several hop-pickers' trains arrived two to three minutes before the departure of the residential trains. The consequence was that those businessmen who allowed themselves just enough time to catch their train without running found themselves, on arrival at the entrance to the Low Level station, confronted by a pandemonium of men, women, children, babies and bundles, none of whom smelled any too sweet. The trouble was partly ameliorated when one of the outer double gates was closed in order to keep those who had come to greet the returning hoppers away from the circulating area.

A NON-STOP TRAIN

The London & Blackwall Railway operated an early non-stop train in an era when trains stopped at most stations. Another curious feature of the line was that its double track was not Up and Down, but each line used alternately by Up and Down trains. This was because it was cable-operated, powered by a stationary steam engine.

A composite coach on the London & Blackwall Railway: first-class passengers are seated inside, while those in third class are required to stand outside. The brake lever is on the right.

As the line had five intermediate stations in about 3½ miles and passed on a viaduct through a densely populated district, it was believed that there was a high danger of burning coke, which the contemporary engines used, flying about among the roofs of the contiguous houses. Thus, to avoid this problem, cable operation was adopted. Experience showed this belief to be false and within nine years of opening it was worked by locomotives.

As the stationary engines were at Minories station and the extension to Fenchurch Street on a rising gradient of 1 in 150, a departing train could gravitate to Minories station, where it was attached to the rope. In the Up direction, this gradient afforded sufficient retardation to dissipate the momentum attained by trains prior to reaching Minories station where the rope ended.

At Blackwall the ropes were attached or detached some distance from the terminus, the line being on a gradient of 1 in 150, the same as Fenchurch Street. The track gauge was 5ft. No seats were provided for third-class passengers, who were required to stand.

The electric telegraph was provided for signalling between the engine houses and the various stations so officials knew when trains started. It was the first railway to be equipped with the electric telegraph from the beginning.

The method of working was unusual. The first coach of a train ran non-stop from one end of the line to the other, a coach being slipped at each station, so the train became shorter and shorter. In the Up direction, each station despatched a coach as soon as the rope started moving, so the complete train was not made up until it reached its destination!

The service was inaugurated on 6 July 1840 and extended to Fenchurch Street about a year later. It offered a popular service, and sometimes twenty-four carriages weighing, with passengers, 200 tons were moved at a time when a normal load for a locomotive was about 50 tons. Hemp ropes lasted about two months and were soon replaced by wire cables.

A FREE BED FOR THE NIGHT

Around 110 years ago, some homeless people were obtaining a free bed for the night. They sought out a siding holding railway carriages and selected one, preferably first class and with lavatory accommodation, to provide the acme of comfort.

To prevent this unauthorised use of a carriage in sidings adjacent to or in large stations, the Lancashire & Yorkshire Railway in 1913 sought Parliamentary powers to enable it to deal with a person from an 'undesirable class' who slept in compartments of railway carriages standing in sidings. It was proposed to permit a penalty to be enforced of up to 40s and to make damages recoverable.

The LYR's Police Superintendent, Frederick Sharp, told the House of Commons Committee that in only one case had he known a vagrant to sleep in a third-class coach. 'They always went into first class compartments and spread cushions on the floor. In one case a verminous person got into a compartment and the result was that the whole carriage had to be disinfected and re-upholstered at a cost of £60.'

A DONKEY ENGINE

In December 1913 enginemen held a strike at Llanelli. During this period, goods traffic for the town was detached at the passenger station and not shunted into the goods shed. Much of the traffic was perishable, so the local tradesmen were pressing for delivery – no sale, no profit. So about midnight, on the suggestion of Inspector Barnes, three of the goods staff, including the inspector himself, went to the fields of the Great Western Docks and obtained a donkey grazing there.

They led it to the goods yard and, with help from the goods staff, wagons were transferred one by one to the goods shed, the task taking a total of about five hours. Each truck and its contents had a gross weight of approximately 10 tons and when a wagon was put in motion by the united efforts of four men and a donkey,

A donkey shunting at Llanelli during the enginemen's strike in December 1913. Men and the donkey started a wagon moving, after which the donkey could continue to pull without too much strain.

once moving, the latter easily hauled it on the level. This showed the slight amount of friction there was with vehicles running on smooth rails compared with an ordinary road.

Draught horses were used for shunting until the 1950s – for instance a horse drew coal wagons to the coal chutes of Bath electricity generating station until April 1953, but the uses of a donkey for railway purposes was rare.

A ROAD-RAIL BUS

Today, the contractors maintaining Britain's railways use road vehicles adapted for running on railways, but this is far from being a new idea. In 1921 a Leyland road motor bus belonging to the North Eastern Railway was converted by that company to run

The North Eastern Railway's Leyland railbus on 19 July 1921, working the York, Copmanthorpe, Strensall and Earswick service.

on rails. The conversion was carried out to discover if, on lines where passenger numbers were low, a service could be operated more economically than with steam power.

On 19 July 1922, bus No. 110 commenced working the service from York to Copmanthorpe, Strensall and Earswick. Manned by a driver and conductor as if running on a highway, single-journey tickets were issued on board so that passengers avoided the trouble of going to a booking office.

The bus seated twenty-six passengers and was powered by a standard 35hp engine.

ANOTHER EARLY RAILBUS

The London, Midland & Scottish Railway opened the luxury Welcombe Hotel at Stratford-upon-Avon on 1 July 1931. To encourage passengers from London to use the LMS route to Stratford, rather than that of the rival Great Western, the LMS used a road-railer to carry them between their station at Blisworth and the hotel.

The road-railer was a twenty-two-seater bus capable of running on either rail or road. It was like an ordinary contemporary bus, except that it had a passenger door on each side. Like the coaches of the period, provision was made for carrying luggage on its roof. Its body was built by Messrs Craven, while Karrier Motors Ltd built the chassis. Powered by a 6-cylinder, 120hp petrol engine, it had a top gear ratio of 7:1 for road use and 4:1 for rail, giving maximum speeds of 60mph and 75mph respectively, though in reality the Ministry of Transport limited its road speed to 30mph like all other heavy vehicles. Petrol consumption was 8mpg on the road and 16mpg on rail, as on the latter less rolling resistance was experienced.

Flanged wheels were fitted to the vehicle's axles and on the outside of these were pneumatic-tyred road wheels. When on a road, the road wheels were locked concentrically to the rail wheels,

The London, Midland & Scottish Railway's rail coach used in 1931 to carry passengers between Blisworth station and its Welcombe Hotel, Stratford-upon-Avon. Note that, unlike a purely road vehicle, doors are provided on both sides.

which, being of smaller diameter, were clear of the ground. On rails, the road wheels were eccentric to the rail wheels. The change could be carried out in two-and-a-half minutes.

It began the service on 23 April 1932, Shakespeare's birthday in the town of his birth, and worked until 2 July 1932. Although a mechanical success, at 7 tons 2cwt it was too heavy for its engine and was withdrawn after the front axle broke.

DRESSING LOCOMOTIVES

About 1900 the policy of decorating locomotives when carrying special passengers was still in place. When King Edward VII and Queen Alexandra travelled from London to Wolferton on their honeymoon, the Great Northern Railway engine No. 284 was painted white with floral decorations by French artists. When the Prince and Princess of Wales returned from their trip around the Empire, the London, Brighton & South Coast Railway engine No. 54 *Empress* drew them from Portsmouth to London. It was adorned with the Royal Arms and Crown and the sides of the cab, splashers, tender and handrails outlined with coloured festoons.

When Lord Roberts returned after the Boer War, the engine heading his train to London was decorated with flags, crests and other devices.

FITTER'S FINANCIAL FORFEITURE

A fitter had the job of scrambling into the boiler of a locomotive undergoing repair to the blower pipe that was situated within. The dome had been removed, and as the fitter entered the boiler through this aperture he became caught by the pocket of his overalls. In his struggle to free himself, the pocket containing his purse was ripped off and fell between the tightly packed boiler tubes.

Many attempts were made to rescue his purse, but all to no avail. Repairs completed, the fire had to be lit for the engine to go back into steam, so the unfortunate fitter sadly saw his money boiled away.

Arguably, he was luckier than some engine cleaners. Sometimes these embryo footplatemen, especially at night, might hide from the foreman and seek forty winks in a locomotive's firebox from which the fire had been removed but was still cosy and warm.

Its use as a bedroom was not an unmitigated success, as there was always the danger that a shovelful of live coal could be thrown on you by an unsuspecting person preparing to start the fire.

SPEED OF BOARDING

Saloon carriages can be filled quicker than compartment coaches because passengers board and then find a seat, whereas with the latter they seek an empty seat before boarding.

DOORS FITTED ONLY ON ONE SIDE

The Tal-y-lyn Railway in mid-Wales, thankfully preserved, had all its platforms on the same side of the track. This meant that the doors on its coaches were only fitted on one side. Another peculiarity was that, other than for passengers boarding at Towyn, the guard issued tickets from a window in his brake van. At Towyn he left the train and issued them from an ordinary booking office. Yet a further peculiarity was that at the period when most railways had just a first and third class, the Tal-y-lyn had no first class, but did have a second and third.

The Glasgow Underground also had platforms on just one side of a coach, so these had doors just on one side and to save money were only painted decoratively on the side seen by the public.

BOGIE CARRIAGES LESS SAFE THAN
SIX-WHEELERS

On 16 June 1919 a London & North Western Railway Blackpool to Birmingham express derailed at Acton Bridge station between Warrington and Crewe, having been off the line for about 120ft. The engine and the first four coaches then rerailed themselves at a V-crossing.

Major Hall, the Board of Trade inspector, said that the fact that the train was composed of six-wheeled coaches instead of bogie vehicles meant that their practically rigid wheelbase caused them to follow a perfectly straight course behind the engine No. 2442, taut couplings keeping them in line. Had the train been composed of bogie vehicles, the bogies would have turned and twisted right and left according to the successive obstructions each bogie met after derailment.

The remaining fourteen coaches of the train derailed on the opposite side of the track and therefore, when they reached the V-crossing, the obstruction could not act as a rerailing ramp.

ACT OF A MISCHIEVOUS YOUTH

In 1842 a mischievous youth started a cattle wagon moving at Northallerton on the Great North of England Railway. Aided by a strong north wind, it travelled as far as Alne, a distance of 18¾ miles, before stopping.

BACK TO TEA & CREAM

Under the general managership of the Great Western Railway of Felix Pole, in 1921 the GWR decided to revert to tea and cream livery for its coaches.

Towards the end of 1908, the tea and cream colours that had given distinction to the company for so many years began to give way to a red-brown tint, but it was generally agreed that this was a mistake. The excuse for the change had been that the new colour would not show the dirt so conspicuously and thus the cost of cleaning be reduced, though whether any economy had been made was never revealed.

Had it not been for a close agreement between the London & South Western Railway and the GWR at the time, it might have been a good idea for the LSWR to have adopted the tea and cream, rather than change from a miserable salmon and brown to dark green.

PARALLEL LIVERY

London, Tilbury & Southend Railway coaches were a teak colour, as were those of the Great Eastern. Both companies ran into Fenchurch Street station, so all the carriages seen there were of the same brown colour. In 1912 the LTSR was taken over by the Midland, which had a red livery, so in due course ex-LTSR coaches were repainted.

In 1919 the Great Eastern also adopted a red livery and, furthermore, the numerals it used for distinguishing the class of travel were similar to the Midland pattern, so this resulted in Fenchurch Street station still having all its coaches in a similar livery.

'NEUTRAL' COACHES

The Tilbury section of the Midland Railway had a number of first-class coaches with the end compartments not marked as to class; these compartments were called 'neutrals'. These coaches were used principally on boat trains to and from Tilbury, most passengers travelling first class. In times of pressure, first-class passengers could be carried in the neutral compartments, while at other times they were available for those with third-class tickets.

8

MISCELLANY

THE GREAT WESTERN CARRIES A
COTTAGE ON ITS WAY TO THE USA

There must have been very few fourteenth-century cottages that have been transported by rail. One of the few examples was around 1930 when a United States' citizen purchased Rose Cottage, Chedworth, Gloucestershire – a typical Cotswold structure with an adjoining barn.

The stones were numbered and packed into boxes and the Great Western Railway then carting the material to Foss Cross station on the Andoversford to Andover line, formerly the Midland & South Western Junction Railway.

From there the sixty-seven wagons were hauled to Brentford and barged down the Thames to the SS *Citizen* in London Docks for transit to the USA. The total weight of the cottage and barn was 475 tons.

NOTICES AMENDED BY SCHOOLBOYS

Before alighting wait until the train stops: Before alighting wait until the rain stops.

Please retain your ticket: Please restrain your ticket.

Do not lean out of the window: Do not leap out of the window.

To lower the window pull strap towards you: To love the widow pull strap towards you.

A Second World War notice – During the blackout, blinds must be pulled down and kept down: During the blackout, blonds must be pulled down and kept down.

AMAZING COINCIDENCE

During the First World War two Australian brothers were in the Australian Artillery. Both were injured in the Battle of Bullecourt and taken to Boulogne Hospital, but neither knew of the other's whereabouts even though they were only two wards apart.

Eventually one brother was moved to a hospital at Weymouth and the other to a hospital in Brighton, still unaware of the other's whereabouts. They eventually met at Charfield station in Gloucestershire, en route to Wootton-under-Edge where they were to convalesce at the home of an uncle.

HOMES NEAR A RAILWAY

When railways were being projected, some landowners hoped to make a good profit by selling their property to the company.

The Great Western Railway usually offered landowners a fair price, but if there was a dispute a public inquiry was held and an arbitrator decided the value.

Three houses in Bathwick Terrace, Bath, were required by the railway. The company offered £2,700, but Mackay, the owner, demanded £3,200. He would have been wise to have accepted the offer: the judge assessed the value of the property at £2,650.

At Kennington, just south of Oxford, Mr Towle constructed a timber and cardboard house on the alignment of the proposed line from Didcot, anticipating a large compensation for being forced to move. He was disappointed!

When the Stonehouse & Nailsworth Railway was being constructed in 1865, a landslip took place above a cutting north of Woodchester, the sliding clay slope causing the foundations of a house above the cutting to slip. In the early stages of its excavation, due to the door frames becoming constantly distorted, the householder took to bed with him all the necessary tools to open his bedroom door in the morning. The slip eventually ceased when springs were drained from the higher ground.

WHY ARE AN ABOVE AVERAGE NUMBER OF CLERGYMEN AND ORGANISTS INTERESTED IN RAILWAYS?

One answer is that in some ways the Church and railways are similar. At a station there is hustle and bustle when a train arrives, followed by calm, quiet and emptiness following its departure. This is not unlike a congregation arriving for a service – probably not with as much hustle, bustle and noise as a station – followed by the emptiness of the building when the service is over.

The regular pattern of church services can be compared with a railway timetable – religious life is not haphazard, it is orderly.

Regarding the link between organists and railways, Michael Doubleday's letter to *The Times* on 13 October 2015 gives a clue. He wrote:

I was for many years the timetable planning manager of British Rail's West Coast Main Line and an amateur composer. When giving talks on how the railway timetable was constructed,

I invariably began by producing a musical score and pointing out that it was in effect a timetable; from personal experience I could also confirm that the processes involved in the production of both are remarkably similar.

RAILWAY TIME

A primitive way of telling the time was to use a sundial. Due to the sun travelling from east to west, this meant that its highest point, noon, was at different times in different parts of the country.

This was of little consequence when the horse provided the fastest means of transport, but when railways increased the speed of travel, and allowed more people to travel faster, the variation of local time caused problems. A railway timetable had to be for a whole area, and could not accommodate local time zones.

In November 1840 the GWR adopted Greenwich as the railway time. This was brought about largely by the electric telegraph apparatus that had been installed on a short section of the GWR in 1839. By 1852 a telegraphic link had been established between an electro-magnetic clock at Greenwich, connected via the Central Telegraph Station of the Electric Time Company in the City of London. This enabled the transmission of a time signal to be made along the railway telegraphic network to other stations and by 1855 time signals from Greenwich could be sent through the railway companies' lines that ran alongside the railways across the length and breadth of Britain.

By 1855, 95 per cent of towns and cities had transferred to Greenwich Mean Time, but it was not until 2 August 1880, when the Statutes (Definition of Time) Act received the Royal Assent, that a unified standard of time for the whole of Great Britain finally achieved legal status.

Before the advent of the telegraph, station masters adjusted their clocks using tables supplied by the railway company to convert local time to London time. Train guards would set their chronometers against the master clock at a London station, locked to avoid being tampered with, and this time was then conveyed by the guard along the system, allowing other stations to have the correct railway time.

INTERESTING RAILWAY CLOCK FACTS

By the mid 1950s there were over 55,000 clocks in service with British Railways. Most railway clocks had 12in diameter dials, and dials larger than 14in are fairly rare.

The London & South Western Railway (and its descendants, the Southern Railway and British Railways Southern Region) favoured fusee clocks with 8in-diameter dials. (A fusee was a conical drum around which, along with the spring's barrel, gut was wound. This device kept the spring's power constant as it unwound.)

THE DANGER OF USING A FREE

SWIMMING POOL

If a railway line had cuttings, material from them could be used to make ramps for overbridges, but if the country being traversed was flat, this option was unavailable. In order to obtain material to create ramps, so-called 'borrow pits' were dug – though in actual fact what was taken out was never replaced!

These pits often filled with water so on a hot day provided tempting swimming pools for the local youths. There was one such pond at Nailsea, just west of Bristol.

On 15 August 1840 Michael Pascoe, aged 16, son of a collier and a non-swimmer, unaware of a 12ft drop from the shallow portion, stepped out of his depth and struggled for air. Henry Weymouth, 17, son of a schoolmaster and also a non-swimmer, attempted to rescue him but he, too, got into difficulties. Both teenagers drowned.

A GIGANTIC PUDDING

The opening of the South Devon Railway from Torre to Paignton on 2 August 1859 was certainly celebrated in style by baking an enormous pudding. Made in eight portions and then put together, it weighed a total of 1½ tons.

The pudding contained 573lb of flour, 382lb of raisins, 191lb of currants, 191lb of bread, 382lb of suet, a 'great number of eggs', 360 quarts of milk, 320 lemons, 95lb of sugar and 144 nutmegs. It cost nearly £50 to make and the pudding was drawn by eight horses to the green where the public dinner took place.

CASH & CARRY

The Scottish railway companies adopted the useful shop parcel system, which avoided a purchaser having to lug round all his or her shopping, but this idea was not taken up in England. A passenger on a shopping trip could buy at a station a packet of labels priced at a penny each. A perforation ran through the centre of each label and, when an item was purchased, you stuck on half the label. Then, when you finished your shopping, you went to the station cloakroom and, upon presenting the half-labels you had retained, were handed your parcels, which the shops had delivered to the station.

THE DOCKERS' UMBRELLA

The Liverpool Overhead Railway, colloquially known as 'The Dockers' Umbrella', was the very first urban elevated electric railway in the world. Another world first was that it used automatic semaphore signals and when these were replaced by colour light signals in 1921, this was yet another first. In 1901 the first escalator to be used by a British railway was installed at Seaforth Sands station.

In order to prevent blocking road entrances to the docks, the line was built 16ft above street level. Columns supported wrought-iron girders placed at 22ft intervals.

The first section, from Dingle to Seaforth Sands, was opened on 6 March 1893. On Grand National Days a special through service was worked over the contiguous electrified Lancashire & Yorkshire Railway line to Aintree. As the L&Y used 600v DC compared with the Liverpool Overhead's 520v DC, the Overhead drivers were instructed to keep their motors running in series when working beyond Seaforth Sands.

The line's closure came in 1956 due to the fact that the system was generally life-expired, had lost traffic to road competition and finance was unavailable for the necessary renewals. It was a loss to Liverpool as, in addition to offering daily transport for dockers, it offered tourists a marvellous view of the docks.

RAILWAY TRAMWAYS

It is not generally known that some railways operated street tramways. One was the Wolverton & Stony Stratford Tramway linking the carriage works of the London & North Western Railway with Stony Stratford. A steam-worked, 3ft 6in-gauge line, it opened on 27 May 1887. The fare was 2d, far cheaper than the 6d charged by its ancestor the horse bus. Workmen were entitled to weekly tickets at 1s and these could be used for four

A scene at the Forester's Arms, Stony Stratford. Time has proved that the car was too long and it has sagged. Haulage is provided by a Thomas Green & Son locomotive of 1887.

journeys daily. A tram engine drew up to three very long double-deck cars, some seating 100 passengers.

The tramway company went into liquidation on 17 July 1919 and as the line was principally used by its workmen, the London & North Western Railway took over the tramway. Following the 1923 Grouping, the line became the property of the London, Midland & Scottish Railway.

The trams were limited to a speed of 8mph and many passengers deserted to the faster motor buses. With the General Strike in 1926, the service was suspended on 4 May and never resumed.

In June 1899 the Great North of Scotland Railway opened a 3ft 6½in-gauge electric tramway to connect its station at Cruden Bay with its hotel. The line carried passengers to the hotel's front

A car on the Great North of Scotland Railway's Cruden Bay Tramway. Laundry and baggage was conveyed behind the driver, with passengers travelling in the saloon.

door, while goods were carried on a spur to the tradesmen's entrance. Hotel guests were carried free, but other passengers were charged.

As all the Great North of Scotland's laundry work was carried out at the hotel, the tramway also carried this. When the branch closed to passengers on 31 October 1932 it became goods only, finally closing when the hotel was requisitioned by the army in March 1941.

The Blackpool & Fleetwood Tramway opened 14 July 1898 on sleepered track. The Lancashire & Yorkshire and London & North Western railways sought powers to build a branch to Cleveleys, but then came to an arrangement with the tramway to have a link at Fleetwood and work wagons over the tramway to Cleveleys. This agreement lasted until 1949.

COPING WITH HOLIDAY CROWDS

In 1919 holiday traffic to Blackpool became almost unmanageable despite the fifteen platforms at Blackpool North and fourteen at Blackpool Central, so on the busiest days, advance booking was introduced to ensure an even flow of passengers. This occurred over the eleven holiday weeks and included day, half-day and evening excursions.

RUSH HOUR IMBALANCE

C.J. Selway, the Great Northern Railway's Superintendent of the Line, revealed that for every 100 passengers conveyed to London in the morning rush hour, two and three-quarter people travelled in the opposite direction. Evening loading was rather better: for each 100 carried to the suburbs, the returning train carried five from the suburbs to inner London.

HOW THINGS HAVE CHANGED

On 22 January 1967 Bulleid Pacifics No. 34102 *Lapford* and No. 34057 *Biggin Hill* worked the Bridport Belle Rail Tour from Waterloo. It made an unscheduled stop at Basingstoke, when a corpse was found in a toilet. It was established that the body had been there from the previous day when the stock had been in normal passenger service. After a short delay, the cadaver was removed and the train proceeded. Today the train would have been held for hours!

LOST VALUABLES

On 4 May 1844, when the Paddington–Oxford train stopped at Slough, a woman called to a porter that she had dropped 'valuables' under the train. The porter assured her that he would have a word with the guard, that the train would draw forward and he would collect the valuables.

The train moved and the porter collected the valuables, everyone craning out of the windows to see what the treasure was. What was it? A 2lb carton of sugar.

IRISH HOME RULE

In October 1883 Fenians attempting to gain Home Rule for Ireland bombed a Paddington–Edgware Road train, injuring sixty-two passengers, but another attack the same month at Charing Cross caused only superficial damage. At Aldersgate in April 1897 one passenger was killed and others severely injured, one receiving fatal injuries.

GONE FOR A BURTON

The opening of railways caused the production of ale in Burton-on-Trent to increase fifty-fold between 1840 and 1900. The industry expanded to take over most of the town centre, which was criss-crossed by a complex network of branch lines and private lines serving the many breweries and maltings. Two of the companies, Bass & Co. and Allsopp & Sons, distributed their products nationally.

Bass & Co. organised an annual excursion for its employees and families to a coastal resort. The first trip only required two trains, but by 1916 no fewer than eighteen were required to carry the 10,000 excursionists.

The local Liberal MP, Michael Thomas Bass, was a financial backer to the Amalgamated Society of Railway Servants founded in 1872 at Derby, and until then any criticism of a railway company was regarded as insubordination.

As his firm sent 500,000 barrels of beer by rail annually, his was a voice of importance. Although the Factory Act of 1811 limited the hours worked in some industries, it did not apply to railway employment. Bass informed the House of Commons that on the Midland Railway, although a driver's standard working day consisted of ten hours, he knew of thirty to forty men who worked almost double that.

As we saw on page 22, the undercroft of St Pancras station, now used for retail purposes etc, was designed originally for Burton beer traffic, the pillars set at such intervals to allow the maximum number of barrels to be stored.

GRAHAM ELLIS

Graham Ellis, an influential figure in the steam preservation movement who helped to save the Steamtown Locomotive Depot at Carnforth, also created the 10¼in narrow-gauge railway on Mull and played a leading part in saving the historic steamship *Sir Walter Scott* sailing on Loch Katrine. During the Second World War he had been a member of the Home Guard and said that his platoon was commanded by Captain Mainwaring's alter ego.

One day, preparing to travel by train to an exercise, the officer lined his men up on the station platform and told them that when their train arrived, they should let the civilians board first. He then commanded the men to board by blowing his whistle. This caused the train to start and left them waiting on the platform.

RAILWAY BIRDS' NESTS

Two wagtails built a nest and reared four young birds in a niche in the framework of a railway carriage that was in daily use. The coach travelled between two stations on the London & South Western Railway, making four journeys a day and covering about a total of 40 miles. The station master at one end often used to see the cock bird waiting with food for the return of his gadabout family.

Thrushes have been known to nest on goods wagons waiting in sidings, but they usually desert when the trucks are moved. On one occasion, however, a pair of thrushes was known to rear a brood in a nest built under the body of a wagon that was in regular use, while the buffer of a passenger coach in daily service was chosen as a nesting site by a blue titmouse.

Robins are notoriously confident birds, but the pair that elected to nest under a railway line displayed real valour. A still more remarkable case is that of a skylark that built its nest under the permanent way between Newmarket and Dullingham, thirty trains thundering immediately over this nest every day.

Birds are commonly said to have no sense of smell, but it was the sense of hearing that must surely have been deficient in the pair of house sparrows that nested inside a station gong that was sounded 100 times every twelve hours.

BOVRIL ADVERTISEMENTS

In the first half of the twentieth century Messrs Bovril used clever and ingenious railway-themed phrases to advertise their products on stations. Some of these were:

Bovril renders express service in emergency.
Luggage in advance but always take Bovril sandwiches.
If you lose your train don't lose your Bovril.

Bovril will carry you further than the train.

Bovril is first class fare.

Guard against chills and colds with Bovril.

Of signal service in sickness – Bovril.

Tourists return in health on Bovril.

No summer excursions without Bovril sandwiches.

Your 'Guard's' name is Bovril.

Fog signals to take Bovril.

A Bovril season gives that first-class feeling.

Refreshment room for Bovril.

Don't spa with our health resort to Bovril.

COALS TO NEWCASTLE

Grimsby is now famed as a fishing port, yet in 1854 Padstow fish were being taken by rail to Lowestoft and Grimsby.

That year, Edward Watkin, general manager of the Manchester, Sheffield and Lincolnshire Railway, travelled to Brixham and prevailed on two or three Brixham trawlers to relocate to Grimsby. They flourished there and Grimsby eventually had the largest fishing fleet in the kingdom.

PURPLE FOR DANGER

Although red is universally adopted as a danger light for railway signals, in some locations purple was used.

The reason was not that it was more conspicuous, but that it was less so and could not be seen until a train was near a lamp.

At places on the coast, such as Dover and Folkestone, a 'Stop' signal that faced the sea showed violet when in the 'On' position so that its red lamp would not be mistaken for the port-side light of a ship. The violet light used on these signals was so feeble that it would be invisible from the sea. Although green signals could be mistaken for green starboard lights, a signal was only pulled 'Off' for a brief period.

GREEN CLEARER THAN RED

A Great Western engine driver who turned his train into the bay platform line at Henley-in-Arden station early on the morning of 25 June 1911 suggested that the green lamp tended to kill an adjacent red light, which consequently could not be seen at so great a distance as it would have been had there been no green light in its vicinity.

A FAST JOURNEY

In 1912, when there were still three classes of rail travel, a motorist explained to a friend how he had missed the boat train at Victoria, but using his car, still caught the Ostend boat at Dover. 'That's nothing,' a Bromley season ticket holder retorted, 'I frequently make my ten-mile journey in a second.'

THE LANCASHIRE & YORKSHIRE RAILWAY

ADVERTISES IN BELGIUM

The Lancashire & Yorkshire Railway advertised its Hull–Zeebrugge ferry extensively in Belgium, Germany and Switzerland. In 1913 passengers on the Belgian State Railways between Ostend and Brussels and Brussels–Antwerp could not fail to notice large hoardings facing the line announcing this service.

THE CONNECTION BETWEEN THE SUEZ
||||||||||||||||||||||||||||||||||||||||||||||||||||||||||||||||||||||||||||||||||||||||||||||||||||||||||||

CANAL AND THE MIDLAND RAILWAY
||||||||||||||||||||||||||||||||||||||||||||||||||||||||||||||||||||||||||||||||||||||||||||||||||||||||||||

On 1 January 1909 the Midland Railway adopted the Train Control System for directing movements of goods and mineral trains – a modified form of a method operated for many years controlling the passage of ships through the Suez Canal.

Initially the Midland Railway used the telegraph for communication, then changed to the telephone as being a much quicker method for Control Officers to issue instructions to signalmen. Brake vans had symbols painted on to identify a train, a signalman gathering particulars as it passed his box. The departure of a train was immediately telephoned to the Head Control Office, so that it held an overview of the situation.

This had the advantage that should the trainmen's hours become excessive, a train could finish short of its destination and traffic sent forward by other services where capacity was available. The Control System eventually included passenger trains. If, for an example, an express was late, this might allow Control to tell a signalman to send a goods train ahead of it. Most of the other main railways adopted the system.

RAILWAY SUPPLIES TOWN WITH GAS
||||||||||||||||||||||||||||||||||||||||||||||||||||||||||||||||||||||||||||||||||||||||||||||||||||||||||||

Until the gas industry was nationalised, gas was usually produced locally by a company or the local authority; however, at Sillouth gas for the town was provided by the North British Railway.

WHERE THERE'S A WILL,
||||||||||||||||||||||||||||||||||||||||||||||||||||||||||||||||||||||||||

THERE'S NOT A WAY
||||||||||||||||||||||||||||||||||||||||||||||||||||||||||||||||||

Amy Moul, a spinster who died in 1913, lived close to Paddington station, but did not study Great Western Railway timetables or she would not have directed an impossibility in her will.

She stipulated that her body should be placed in a perfectly simple white coffin, which was to be placed in a leaden coffin with heavy weights, 'Amy Moul, London' to be stamped on top and taken down by the midnight train to Falmouth Station. The next morning, if fine, it was to leave the landing stage at 7 o'clock and be taken out to sea, no further than necessary; four men and a chaplain to take the coffin in a boat; the chaplain to receive his ordinary fee, and each man an additional pound as a present from her.

The problem was that the midnight train from Paddington was not due at Falmouth until 10.22 a.m., making it impossible to leave the landing stage at 7.00 a.m.

The nearest approach to her timetable would have been sending her coffin by the 9.50 p.m. from Paddington, due Falmouth at 7.03 a.m., allowing the funeral ship to get under way about 7.30 a.m. She may have made the timing error if she knew that the Cornish Riviera Express reached Falmouth in six hours twenty minutes from Paddington and thus was under the impression that all trains to Falmouth travelled at this speed.

A ROBINSON CRUSOE RAILWAY
||||||||||||||||||||||||||||||||||||||||||||||||||||||||||||||||||||||||||||||||

In 1913 Whale Island in Portsmouth Harbour was government property and reserved by the Admiralty for a gunnery school.

The island had a standard-gauge railway consisting of a mile of main line and half a mile of branches and sidings. Before becoming an isolated Robinson Crusoe Railway, it had been joined to the government railway in Portsmouth Dockyard and through it to the London, Brighton & South Coast Railway and London & South Western Railway. Whale Island had been connected with the remainder of the dockyard lines by a viaduct across the harbour, but in 1896 the government demolished the viaduct to create privacy.

Regarding the Crusoe Railway, G.A. Sekon wrote in the *Railway & Travel Monthly*:

> The permanent way is in several places embedded in the soil, but the traffic is light and engine drivers are forbidden to rival the speed of the 'Cornish Riviera', or other notable feats of the GWR as their engines have a tendency to leave their appointed paths. The curves, too, are exceedingly sharp. An hydraulic traversing jack is carried on one of the engines and is very useful. The steepest bank has a gradient of 1 in 25.

The line possessed two engines, a 0-4-0ST and a 0-6-0T, both in a livery of dark green lined with red and yellow. When either engine needed repair it was carried to the dockyard in a lighter.

A four-wheeled passenger van was used by the captain to meet his boat at 8.45 a.m. and take him to his private station in the garden of the office block containing his office. This was the only station with a platform, elsewhere a ladder carried on the carriage was used to assist entry or exit at stopping points.

WHAT THE EYE DOESN'T SEE

In the early days of railways, wagons of coal used to be sheeted because it was considered *infra dig* for the aristocratic iron roads to convey such plebeian material as 'black diamonds'.

The general sheeting of coal trucks fell into disuse by 1850 and tarpaulins were reserved just to protect material that would spoil or deteriorate by exposure to the weather.

George Stephenson's prophecy that dung would soon be conveyed by rail was speedily fulfilled and whole train loads of noxious material – such as London house and street refuse – were sent openly on the various railway lines radiating from the metropolis.

Early in the twentieth century it was recognised that many dangerous germs could be distributed around the country by the passage of truckloads of such rubbish and be a menace to the health of the districts through which it was conveyed. Hampstead Borough Council provided sheets for covering its refuse despatched by the Midland Railway. So large was the volume sent away by rail that Hampstead Borough Council possessed several hundred sheets to cover the refuse wagons.

WARTIME ADVERTISING

In the First World War the London & North Western Railway, like many other railways, supplied motor lorries and vans to the army, often with advertisement placards still on them. An LNWR railwayman at the front wrote facetiously to Euston: 'Tell Mr ****[the bill inspector] that our motors over here require new bills on them.'

'INHERENT VICE' IN A PIANO

Lawyers have unusual expressions to express out-of-the-way ideas that need special pleading to obtain recognition. The term 'inherent vice' is one that the legal profession can fall back on when all other ingenious defences are of no avail. The application of the expression to explain some otherwise inexplicable action of an animal is allowable.

The Great Western Railway solicitors used the idea successfully when a consignment of pianos was damaged because of 'inherent vice', not of a locomotive, or wagon, but of the pianos.

The plaintiff's idea of damage was more far-fetched than that of the defence, as he alleged that the damage to the piano was caused by steam from a passing locomotive seeping into a closed van and creating damp. No proof was offered for this assertion, while the GWR suggested that the pianos had been sent off too soon after they had been polished and a change in temperature on a cold night would have caused the damp to come out of the unhardened polish.

After considering the evidence, the judge stated that of the two probabilities, that of 'inherent vice' suggested by the GWR appealed to him most strongly and judgement was given in favour of that company.

PRETTY AS A PICTURE

In 1915 the Metropolitan Railway revived a vogue common on the line thirty-five years earlier, namely the displaying of advertisements on the backs of tickets. The 1915 revival proposed that the advertisements should be of so artistic a character that passengers would be loath to surrender them to the ticket collector at their journey's end.

It was hoped that the ticket examiner would not cause passengers to miss their trains by spending too long examining the artistic pictures on the reverse of the tickets.

A TRAIN AND ZEPPELIN RACE

In the First World War Zeppelin raids were not infrequent and during one of these attacks there was a neck-to-neck race between the airship and a Great Eastern Railway train near Bury St Edmunds. As the train rushed along at top speed, the Zeppelin hurled five bombs at the speeding train below. All the missiles fell wide of the mark and the train steamed into Bury St Edmunds unharmed.

The reporter commented that he hoped that the engine driver signalled his escape by a loud derisive crow on his whistle.

LACK OF APPRECIATION

John Chiddy was foreman of Birchwood Quarry, situated between Bristol and Keynsham. Just before 2.00 p.m. on 31 March 1876, an Up passenger train dislodged a large stone from the quarry's stack beside the line and fouled the Down track. Knowing that the approach of the Down Flying Dutchman was imminent, John tried to shift the obstruction. His efforts seemed to be in vain, but then, as the express was almost upon him, he shifted the rock but at the cost of his life for the engine struck him before he could jump clear. In due course, the train, which had been travelling at 50mph, stopped and a collection was made.

At the point where John had saved it, the Flying Dutchman had been on a ledge high above the River Avon and, had it become derailed, would most certainly have plunged into the river, resulting in a considerable loss of life. How much did those grateful passengers give? Just £3 17s 0d – precious little compensation for a wife and seven children who had lost their father, not to mention their breadwinner.

Lord Elcho was so incensed that he took up the case in Parliament and declared that if a man risked his life to save others, he should do so 'with the consciousness that his family would not be dependent on charity or the workhouse'. The Chancellor of the Exchequer explained that he had no fund to help such people. However, the ensuing press publicity resulted in an account being opened in Bath and another in Bristol, the Bank of England contributing £10 when informed that two of its officials were on the train with a large quantity of gold.

The total collection of £400 purchased ½ acre of land on which the six-bedroom Memorial Cottage was built in what is now Memorial Road on the Hanham bank of the Avon.

The inscription on Memorial Cottage, Memorial Road, Hanham, originally provided for the widow of John Chiddy.

The smallholding provided the family with a living. The north side of the house bears a plaque carrying the inscription: 'Erected AD 1877 by public subscription for the widow and family of John Chiddy who was killed by an express train whilst removing a large stone from the metals of the Great Western Railway near Conham, March 31st 1876.'

A RAILWAY THAT OFFERED A FREE RIDE

Before a railway was permitted to carry paying passengers it had to be inspected by a Board of Trade official.

However, as the Liskeard & Caradon Railway was built to serve copper mines and quarries, no such check was necessary. In 1860 the company decided to accede to demand and start carrying passengers. It was not allowed to charge fares, but could charge for umbrellas or walking sticks, so when passengers paid for the carriage of one of these implements, they were given a free pass.

Naturally the company did not wish to be held responsible for the expense of any mishap to a passenger, so notices were exhibited reminding passengers that:

> all passes are issued gratuitously, but solely on the considerations that the use of any free pass shall be taken as evidence of an agreement with the Directors that neither the Company, or the Directors, or their servants are to be responsible for any injury or damage which may occur to any person travelling by a free pass through accident, delay, or otherwise whether occasioned by any act or neglect of the Company or its servants or otherwise, or for the loss or damage to property however caused.

RAILWAYS TAKE THE CREAM OF
STRAWBERRY TRAFFIC

Until the 1960s, the transport of strawberries was an important traffic for five or six weeks in June and early July, partly because it was the earliest English fruit to mature and because of its delicious flavour was greatly in demand.

The Tamar district provided the first strawberries of the season, with special trains from Bere Alston, Bere Ferrers and Tavistock. The next strawberries came from Hampshire: Swanwick, Botley, Burlesdon, Wickham, Sholing, Netley, Eastleigh, Fareham and Woolston.

Some pickers actually camped in the strawberry fields and were paid a penny for each chip basket picked, a full basket weighing about 4lb. In 1914, 3 million baskets were sent annually from the Swanwick area.

Before the season began, the London & South Western Railway collected 600–700 passenger-luggage, milk and other vans fitted with vacuum brakes and installed tiers of shelves to pack in the maximum number of baskets in the minimum space. When there were not enough vans available, the LSWR used old excursion fourteen-coach set passenger trains, the baskets being placed on the seats, racks and floors. It was an expensive alternative as they did not hold as much fruit as the vans.

In 1914 Swanwick averaged about 100,000 baskets daily, the heaviest day sending 118,000 baskets, about 227 tons, with twenty-six baskets being reckoned as a hundredweight. Swanwick employed 100 additional men: two inspectors, ten clerks, fifty porters and thirty boys, the latter loading the fruit as they were able to crawl in between the shelves and pack in the furthest corners. As many of the local inhabitants were engaged in strawberry work, lodgings were scarce, so the LSWR provided a cook house and dining tent, with meals supplied at cost. Each van was in charge of a checker, whose job it was to check the consignment notes while the two lads loaded. Carts drawn by donkeys, mules and horses lined up for nearly a mile to unload, the traffic being regulated by LSWR policemen.

Botley averaged 50,000 baskets daily and employed fifty extra staff: a foreman, six clerks, thirty porters and thirteen loading boys. Burlesdon averaged a daily 30,000 baskets. The special trains were marshalled at Bevois Park Sidings near Southampton and picked up loads from various stations, and from Eastleigh ran fast to Willesden or another junction. The first special train of the day carried traffic to the North of England and Scotland. The heaviest special consisted of thirty vehicles.

PROTECTING THE RAILWAY FROM

ETON SCHOLARS

When the bill for building a branch line from Slough to Windsor was being promoted, Eton College, afraid of boys sneaking up to London and enjoying its depravities, had a clause inserted that if the Great Western Railway failed to keep a sufficient number of police or other officers on the line to prevent access by pupils, the headmaster could appoint two officers or servants for the purpose and charge the cost of their wages against the company.

A WHITE LOCOMOTIVE

A London & North Western Railway locomotive superintendent, Francis Webb, a pupil of Francis Trevithick, was a lover of compound engines. This was a steam-saving idea whereby steam was used twice: first in two high-pressure cylinders and then again in a larger version. Although excellent for stationary work, the idea was not generally successful when used on locomotives.

Webb knew that an engine with only a single driving wheel ran more smoothly than a coupled engine, so some of his compound engines had the 2-2-2-2 wheel arrangement – really double singles – high-pressure steam driving one set of wheels and low-pressure steam the other. Unfortunately, sometimes when starting from a station, the valve setting was such that one set of driving wheels went clockwise and the other set anticlockwise, so the train went nowhere.

Compound No. 2094 *Queen Empress* was sent to the Chicago Exhibition in 1893, where she gained a Gold Medal for excellence of workmanship and later hauled a train of LNWR coaches from Chicago to New York. To celebrate Queen Victoria's Diamond Jubilee, 2-2-2-2 compound No. 2053 *Greater Britain* was painted in red and No. 2054 *Queen Empress* in white.

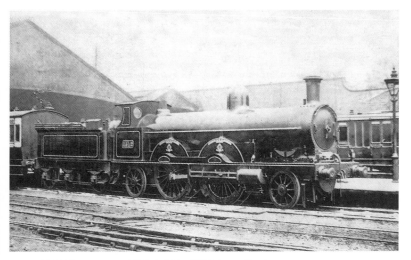

Webb's compound 2-2-2-2 No. 1512 *Henry Dent*.

Altogether Webb built several hundred compounds, none absolutely reliable and some like the eight Greater Britain class of 1891–94, positively bad. Following Webb's forced resignation in 1904, his successor, George Whale, withdrew most of the compounds within three years. Conversely, Webb's 'simple' engines were excellent, gave reliable service and lasted until withdrawn by British Railways in the 1950s.

ONE TRAIN, DIFFERENT SPEEDS

It is a curious fact that when a train is accelerating, or braking, a person at the front and another at the rear will pass a certain point at different speeds. If a train 990ft in length commences climbing Honiton Incline at 75mph and passes the summit at 25mph, an observer in the last coach will take eighteen seconds longer for the climb than the person in the first coach.

IS IT A PUBLIC OR A PRIVATE RAILWAY?

Between Uphall and Livingstone on the North British Railway's Glasgow–Edinburgh line was a 1½-mile-long branch line called the Bangour (Private) Railway. It was private, yet public!

It could be called 'private' because it was constructed and owned by the Edinburgh District Lunacy Board, when in 1900 it began the construction of an asylum at Bangour. It was also 'public' as the authority allowed the public to use it. The line was worked by the North British Railway for 50 per cent of the gross receipts. It rose from the junction with the main line towards Bangour, the steepest gradient being 1 in 88. As the engine carried the single-line staff, signals were unnecessary.

Opened on 19 June 1905, the intermediate station at Deechmont was designated a public station, but Bangour was private, the

An ex-Metropolitan Railway 4-4-0T at Watchet when the West Somerset Mineral Railway was reopened 4 July 1907.

public being admitted as a privilege, not by right, and no goods traffic could be taken to or from Bangour except that of the asylum.

When opened, the daily service was three passenger and one goods trains each way, plus an extra passenger train on Saturdays. During the First World War the asylum was taken over by the War Office as a military hospital to accommodate 1,300 sick or wounded, the branch being used by ambulance trains. The line closed on 4 May 1921.

FROM LONDON'S UNDERGROUND
TO RURAL SOMERSET

When the Metropolitan Railway was electrified, its 4-4-0 tank engines became redundant and were sold for use elsewhere, one of these locations being Somerset.

In the mid-nineteenth century a railway was built from Watchet Harbour to iron ore mines on the Brendon Hills. Traffic was satisfactory at first but then declined to such an extent that the line was closed on 7 November 1898. In 1907 the Somerset Mineral Syndicate reopened the mines and leased the West Somerset Mineral Railway from its owners, the Ebbw Vale Company.

On Sunday, 30 June 1907, ex-Metropolitan Railway 4-4-0T No. 37 arrived via the Great Western Railway and was transferred to the mineral line by a temporary connection at Kentsford, south of Watchet. From there, with two wagons of passengers, it ran to Watchet by gravity. The following day a wagon of new sleepers was drawn by horses to Roadwater and on 4 July an excursion was arranged to Comberow behind No. 37, passengers sitting on benches placed in open wagons.

Production from the mines was disappointingly low, so only one daily goods train was run and on some days no trip was made. The syndicate was wound up on 24 March 1910 and No. 37 sold for £200. On 24 July 1910 the engine and twenty-one wagons were transferred to the GWR at Kentsford for onward removal.

ROBBING PETER TO PAY PAUL

The aphorism 'robbing Peter to pay Paul' was changed on the Midland Railway to 'robbing the main line to gas the branch train'. Every morning when the Hemel Hempstead branch train arrived at Harpenden, a porter took a hose and secured it to the gas cylinder of a main-line train standing at No. 5 platform. Checking that the gauge shown on the main-line coach revealed that it had a good supply of gas, he coupled the other end to the branch coach standing at No. 4 platform.

When a sufficient quantity of gas had flowed into the branch coach cylinder to equalise the pressure, the connection was withdrawn. This method of gassing saved working a gas cylinder wagon to and from Harpenden for the purpose of charging the branch train.

WHY THE DEADMAN'S HANDLE FAILED TO

STOP A TRAIN FOR A DEAD MAN

The deadman's handle was devised to ensure the absolute safety of a train should its driver fail to give attention to his duties.

In 1916 the death of a motorman on the London, Brighton & South Coast Railway was enquired into by the Coroner's Jury at Penge. The guard stated that his passenger train left Crystal Palace station at 2.42 p.m. and should have then stopped at Gipsy Hill but ran through the station. He correctly applied the brake and brought it to a halt ¼ mile beyond the platform. On proceeding to the cab to ascertain the reason for not calling at the station, he found the driver missing. A search found his body in Crystal Palace Tunnel. Why had the deadman's handle failed to stop the train when the driver left the cab?

A motor inspector discovered that a small wedge had been inserted to the control handle to keep the train running without the necessity of the motorman physically holding it down, rendering the supposed security of the deadman's handle null.

No explanation was given of how the driver came to be on the track, but it was imagined that he was leaning far out of the window, struck the side of the tunnel and was dragged out through the window.

CAPTURING A RAILWAY LOCOMOTIVE

On 1 August 1852 a dispute arose between the Great Northern Railway and the Midland Railway regarding traffic to Nottingham. Before it was settled, a train from King's Cross was drawn into the Midland's Nottingham station by a GNR locomotive.

MR officers believed it was time to take a firm stand and so arranged for a number of MR engines to completely block in the GNR locomotive. The GNR driver made a desperate attempt to get his engine out, but failed and was greatly embarrassed to see his engine taken to an old shed and the rails leading to it lifted, thus preventing any escape.

Several months later, and only on the production of documents to prove that his engine had been hired from the Ambergate Railway by the GNR, was the locomotive released.

A similar event occurred at Havant in 1858. The London & South Western Railway advertised that it would open its new line to Portsmouth via Petersfield on 1 January 1859.

Anticipating friction with the rival London, Brighton & South Coast Railway, which also served Portsmouth and over whose track it had running powers between Havant and Portsmouth, in order to ensure that the service would work well, the LSWR announced a trial run on 28 December 1858. The LSWR train was scheduled to arrive at Havant at 10.00 a.m., but actually arrived at 7.00 a.m. The LBSCR was prepared and had placed an engine of its own completely blocking the junction, its wheels chained to the rails and padlocked.

The battle was finally settled in a law court and the first LSWR train ran over the new line to Portsmouth on 24 January 1859.

BAILIFFS SEIZING LOCOMOTIVES

In the early days of railways, bailiffs frequently distrained on locomotives due to impecunious companies not paying debts for locomotives, rolling stock etc. Such an event was less common in later years when railways had become economically stronger, but in June 1908 an express engine at a London terminus was held by a bailiff on account of a debt.

An employee of that railway had met with an accident that disabled him from employment for several weeks. He claimed compensation, but the company denied responsibility. The case was taken to court and an award made in favour of the employee. Sadly, the solicitor acting for the railway company died before the compensation was actually paid and unfortunately the relevant department of the railway overlooked payment.

After several weeks, as the employee's solicitor had not received the money, he assumed that the railway was refusing to pay and issued an execution. The bailiff went to the railway company's offices to demand the money and, failing to receive it immediately, mounted an engine in the station and dared its removal until the sum was paid.

This distraining of the express engine caused a commotion and after a few explanations the money was forthcoming and the locomotive released.

AN ENGINE TUMBLES DOWN A HOLE

On 22 September 1892 a goods train was shunting at Lindall between Barrow and Ulverston on the Furness Railway when driver Thomas Postlethwaite was horrified to see a portion of the embankment subsiding and the ballast slipping away from below the sleepers. The footplate crew sensibly left 0-6-0 No. 115 and were wise to do so because almost immediately afterwards the rails, together with the locomotive and tender, sank into a hole 30ft deep. The engine descended chimney-first, so the tender was not so far embedded and eventually recovered, but despite efforts, the locomotive sank lower and lower into an old ironstone mine and remains there to this day, as does Thomas Postlethwaite's jacket and gold watch.

THE AFFECTION SHOWN TO
THE BROAD GAUGE

In 1892 the Portreeve of Ashburton despatched the last broad-gauge train to leave Ashburton in black crêpe, and thus dressed in mourning it accomplished its final journey to Totnes. Similarly sad at its passing, at Exeter a gentleman stood by the side of the *Iron Duke*, which had brought a train from Bristol, and delivered an oration on the benefits of the broad gauge.

WORLD TRAVEL OF A PENNY
METROPOLITAN DISTRICT RAILWAY TICKET

On 29 August 1915 penny third-class railway ticket No. 4304, Series 31 was purchased from an automatic machine at Earl's Court by a soldier in the Border Regiment. In due course he wrote this poignant letter to the Earl's Court station master telling him of the ticket's adventures:

> Out of sheer curiosity I am writing to know if to your knowledge this following constitutes a record for the number of miles one

of your railway tickets has travelled. I got the ticket from a machine at Earl's Court in August 1915, but owing to meeting a friend at the moment, we sent off together without using it. I next found it in my pocket the next week when I am on a transport boat bound for the Dardanelles. I kept it with me during my time I was there, after which I sent into hospital at Malta. From Malta I went to Egypt and afterwards to France. On July 1st [1916], in a charge I got wounded, and eventually arrived in England on July 9th, bringing with me the ticket which I have enclosed. Perhaps, by some chance, some soldier may have done the same thing, more or less, with one of your tickets and has recorded it to you. I should be very interested to know if such is the case, or that mine holds the record up to the present. Trusting you will excuse pencil, as ink is not allowed in bed, and I am still in bed with my wounds.

THE IMPORTANCE OF HORSEPOWER

During the nineteenth century horses were used to haul delivery vehicles, shunt wagons when a locomotive was unavailable and even on a few branches to actually haul trains. From 1901 motor vehicles began to replace horses for delivery, but even in 1914 the eleven largest railway companies owned almost 26,000 horses.

Stables were sometimes two storeys high, with a ramp leading to the upper floor. Although most of these premises were well ventilated, those for the horses that shunted the fish siding at Birmingham Snow Hill were in the tunnel south of the station and so rarely saw the light of day.

Horse-keepers became very fond of their animals, sometimes visiting them on their day off, and during a strike period, always kept them well fed.

At Nationalisation in 1948, British Railways still owned approximately 9,000 horses, mostly delivering goods around

Tommy, the shunting horse, at Newmarket in October 1961.

towns. BR's last horse was a 24-year-old named Charlie who retired from shunting duties at Newmarket on 21 February 1967.

WICKER BASKETS

In 1883 the London & North Western Railway purchased a basket company at Aylesbury, the railway constructing a larger factory. Land for its branch from Cheddington to Aylesbury had been purchased for double track but, as only single had been laid, the unused space was used for growing osiers. From 1893 until the mid 1920s production averaged about 2,000 baskets annually, ranging from large hampers with a cubic capacity of 22 cu. ft, to waste paper baskets and trays for correspondence. In addition to osiers from local beds, supplies were railed in from other LNWR lines including Oxford–Cambridge and those in Warwickshire and Staffordshire. In the late 1930s the local beds fell into disuse and all osiers were brought in by rail until 31 December 1947, when the factory closed.

ZEPPELINS FOLLOW RAILWAYS

In the First World War Zeppelins found railways helpful to navigation and would often follow a railway, such as the Great Western westwards, or the London & North Western northwards.

The aluminium from a shot-down Zeppelin was given to the London & North Western Railway to be made into pipe racks, shoe lifts, ash trays, pen holders and other items to raise money for its staff who had joined the forces.

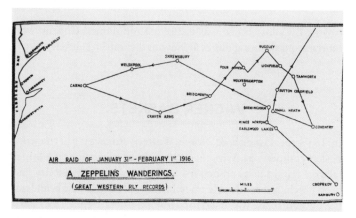

Map showing a Zeppelin's wanderings, mainly following railways, 31 January to 1 February 1916.

A RAILWAY CONTRACTOR'S METHOD OF

ENFORCING PAYMENT

In 1916 James Ramsay died in Bournemouth at an advanced age. He was believed to be the last survivor of those connected with the Arbroath & Forfar Railway, a portion of which was opened as early as January 1839. James Ramsay had been station master at Arbroath from 1862 until 1890, when he retired from railway service.

One of his reminiscences recorded by D.D. Buchan concerned a length of line, later to become a portion of the Caledonian Railway's main line to Aberdeen. Buchan wrote:

> On the opening of the section of the Scottish North Eastern Railway from Friockheim Junction to Limpit Mill – or 'Lampit' as locally known – Mr Ramsay was put on the staff at Fordoun station, and on the day the various stations on the section were manned, an unusual incident took place.
>
> A special train was run from the south, picking up the required men, and then putting them down at the newly completed stations. On the train nearing the big wooden viaduct which had been constructed over the North Esk Valley, south of Fordoun, the driver was astonished to see the bridge-contractor's men standing on the railway and waving a red flag. He stopped, and the contractor said he had not been paid for building the viaduct, and would not allow the train to cross it until he had been paid all that was due to him. To enforce his contention, he had taken up some of the rails. Arguments and expostulations were in vain and the men had to get out and make their way to their respective stations in the best way they could. The contractor was paid in full after four or five days' delay. Traffic was then begun, but the incident caused considerable annoyance as well as local amusement.

A RAILWAY FARM

As part of the effort to become more self-sufficient food-wise in the First World War, the Great Eastern Railway purchased a farm at Bentley, near Ipswich, and between 24 October 1917 and 23 October 1918 conducted experiments in conjunction with the National Utility Poultry Society to discover the breed of hen that was the most prolific egg producer.

WHAT HAPPENED TO HORSES IN A

FIRST WORLD WAR AIR RAID?

Police summonsed a London & North Western Railway carter who left his horse unattended during an air raid. The LNWR then issued instructions on how to deal with this situation: a carter could seek shelter, but was required to leave the brake on, chain the wheel and secure the horses by drawing their heads towards the knees by tying a restraining rope through the bit and securing the other end below the horses' knees.

CLOSING/OPENING YO-YO

The Bristol–Portishead branch has had more closings and openings than average. It closed to passenger traffic on 7 September 1964, but continued to be used by goods. To avoid traffic problems due to too many spectators arriving by road, Ashton Gate was reopened for football specials on 29 September 1970, but this ceased in 1977 when Parson Street took over. Then on 7 October 1977, thirteen years after closure to regular passenger traffic, a special DMU carried pupils from Gordano School on a day return trip from Portishead to Bath.

Two trains at Ashton Gate, 7 June 1960: Class 3MT 2-6-2T No. 82037 with the 2.15 p.m. Portishead–Bristol Temple Meads, and a diesel multiple-unit working the 2.30 p.m. Temple Meads–Portishead.

Goods traffic ceased on 3 August 1981, but the line was mothballed rather than lifted in anticipation that with the opening of the Royal Portbury Dock goods traffic might become economical.

Billy Graham's religious gathering took place at Bristol City's football ground on 12–19 May 1984 and Ashton Gate was again reopened to cater for the special trains arriving. In 1985, as part of the GWR 150 celebrations, steam-hauled and DMU passenger trains ran between Bristol and Portishead.

With the development of Royal Portbury Dock, a need was felt for rail access, so the line was put in working order to Pill and a spur built to the dock. This line opened officially on 21 December 2001.

The road journey between Portishead and Bristol is horrendous at peak hours and there is a strong desire to reopen the branch to passenger traffic, but this is not as simple as it sounds. Currently, the signalling Parson Street Junction–Portishead is for freight traffic, not passenger; the permanent way from Pill to Portishead needs re-laying and stations to be built at Portishead and Pill. The line is expected to reopen to passenger traffic in 2024.

ARGUMENTS FOR AND AGAINST THE USE
OF FIXED DISTANT SIGNALS

For: saves the cost of wire, fittings etc, as on a single line where trains do not pass through stations at speed, there is little object in informing a driver the position of the home signal.

Against: loses the railway meaning of the word 'signal' and makes it merely a sign. It could be a trap for a driver because a fixed distant remaining constantly at Danger conveys no changing intimation, so a driver, knowing what it indicates, is tempted to ignore it and is therefore dispossessed of the protection afforded by an operated distant signal.

TIMES HAVE CHANGED

Until recent years, it was unusual for most British children to begin school until they were 5 years of age. In 1918 it was thought newsworthy to record that a season ticket had been taken out at Brixham to enable a 4-year-old boy to attend school at Torquay – a distance of 7¼ miles. It was not recorded, but implied, that the lad would have undertaken the journey on his own, including changing trains at Churston.

IT DOESN'T PAY TO CHEAT

A RAILWAY COMPANY

On 23 February 1918 Robert Hardy handed to the Parcels Office Waterloo a black Gladstone bag to be forwarded to 'James, Hotel Metropole, Ilfracombe'. He paid the 1s 7d fee and was given a receipt 'James, Ilfracombe' bearing a counter-sheet number. His bag duly arrived at Ilfracombe but could not be delivered as no Hotel Metropole existed.

On 11 March Hardy called at Waterloo and preferred a claim of £23 10s 0d against the London & South Western Railway for the cost of a new Gladstone bag and contents. He claimed that a new brown leather bag had been addressed to 'Hardy, Cloak Room, Ilfracombe' and that he had purchased it at Harrod's on 9 February. He said that he had travelled from Waterloo to Ilfracombe on 27 February, had personally applied for the missing bag and had returned to London the same day.

When the black bag was opened at Ilfracombe it contained old and dirty clothes, a mouse trap, some pieces of wire, an old pair of carpet slippers and other articles of no value.

On inspection, it was found that the counter-sheet number held by Hardy had been partly erased, the letters 'ames' rubbed out and amended to read 'J. Hardy, Ifracombe'.

The LSWR found his story to be a tissue of lies: Harrod's had not sold a Gladstone bag during February and the first train from Waterloo–Ilfracombe was not due to arrive until thirty-four minutes after the departure of the last train to Waterloo, so it would have been impossible for him to have made the trip in a day.

Hardy was sentenced to five years' penal servitude.

THE LONG WAY ROUND

Torrington and Portsmouth Arms stations in Devon are only 9 miles apart as the crow flies, yet although they are on the same main line, the distance between them by rail is 25 miles!

GUARDING IMPORTANT BRIDGES

During the First World War garrisons were stationed on both banks of the Firth of Forth and the Firth of Tay to protect the bridges from sabotage. Had they been destroyed, apart from preventing the passage of trains, the navigable channels would have been blocked by the fallen spans.

NO SMOKING

In 1842 a passenger, despite a warning, defiantly continued to smoke in a London & Birmingham Railway carriage.

The guard ordered the offender to leave the train at a rural station and instructed the staff there that on no account was he to be allowed to continue his journey to London that day.

The guard, on being remonstrated with, observed that he himself was required to obey orders, or he would be liable to suspension or a heavy fine.

Although smoking was initially banned in railway carriages, the Great Eastern was one of the first railways to provide accommodation for smokers when in 1858 it constructed some first-class smoking saloons. By about 1920 the majority of passengers smoked so instead of labelling most compartments 'Smoking', it was more economical to label a few 'Non-Smoking' and permit smoking in others, as non-smokers had complained of smoke in those not labelled 'Smoking'.

THE VINEGAR LINE

Before the days of the Light Railways Act of 1896, it was difficult for a private firm to obtain sanction for building a private railway even a few yards in length if it crossed a public highway, or necessitated the acquisition of property under compulsory purchase powers.

In 1870 Messrs Hill, Evans & Company of the Vinegar Works, Worcester, whose premises were ½ mile from the GWR line, sought powers to build a line and the Worcester Railway Act was passed that year. Other firms whose property adjoined the line used it on payment to Hill, Evans. The line, officially the Lowesmoor Tramway, was better known as 'the Vinegar Branch'.

Unusually, the road traffic over the ungated level crossings was governed by railway-type signals. The Shrub Hill Road crossing had two signals: one for road traffic in one direction, and another for that in the opposite direction, both worked by the same lever. As the arms on the posts pointed the same way, it meant that one was on the correct and the other on the 'wrong' side.

The street outside MacKenzie & Holland's signal works had a post with two signals at right angles: one for the road and the other for the railway. Both arms were interlocked so that it was impossible for both to be off at the same time. This signal was provided by MacKenzie & Holland.

As it crossed three roads on the level, it was important that no runaways occurred and, in addition to wagons in sidings having their brakes applied, sprags were required to be inserted through the spokes of their wheels. On the upward journey two brake vans were required to be at the rear to guard against any breakaways. The maximum load for the branch was twelve vehicles, subject to the gross weight of the twelve not exceeding 104 tons, exclusive of the two brake vans.

THE SOLWAY VIADUCT
IIIIIIIIIIIIIIIIIIIIIIIIIIIIIIIIIIIIIIIIIIIIIIIIIIIIIIIIIIIIIIIII

One of the longest water crossings in Britain was the Solway Viaduct, its principal purpose being to carry West Cumberland iron ore from the mines to the Lanarkshire steel works. The line opened to goods and mineral traffic on 13 September 1869 and to passengers on 8 August 1870.

The 1,940yd Solway Viaduct was carried on 193 cast-iron piers, each supporting 30ft spans. The rails were set 35ft above low water. It proved a costly structure to maintain as in the winter of 1875–76 ice formed inside the 1ft-diameter, cast-iron columns and created cracks, while in January 1881 ice floes demolished forty-five piers and caused girders to collapse. Lack of funds meant that it was not reopened until 1 May 1884. In post-First World War years it again needed repairs, but the cost of these was not justified as the steel mills had changed to using Spanish ore. The viaduct was closed from 1 September 1921 but left *in situ*, and it became an illegal footpath to licensed hospitality denied to Scotsmen on a Sunday. A barbed wire fence was erected, but this was no barrier to the enterprising Celt and the weekly promenades continued until eventually a Sunday bus service between Annan and Carlisle rendered this walk unnecessary. The viaduct was demolished between 1933 and 1935.

BATH WATER BY RAIL
IIIIIIIIIIIIIIIIIIIIIIIIIIIIIIIIIIIIIIIIIIIIIIIIIIIIIIIIIIIIIIIII

The Great Western Railway had traffic carrying brine from Droitwich to Great Malvern, but this stopped at the beginning of the First World War. Adjacent to the railway station at Great Malvern was a large hydropathic hotel owned by a German, interned at the start of the conflict. A feature of the treatment was brine baths, and two wooden railway wagons owned by the German were used to transport it. At the north end of the Down platform was a siding with a turntable at its end. At right angles to this siding and abutting on to the turntable was a railway in a tunnel below the hotel grounds and leading to the hotel itself. In addition there was a private covered way from the hotel grounds to the platform. The war stopped this activity but the wagon full of brine was kept in the siding for six years. The brine preserved the wood, but as the wooden top was not covered by brine, this rotted. When the hotel closed, the building was purchased and became a school.

THE HOME GUARD

For the first two and a half years of the First World War, British railways were guarded carefully and vulnerable spots continued to be placed under observation for some months following the Armistice in 1918. Guard duty was assigned to the Territorials, but as insufficient men could be spared, volunteer railwaymen and others filled the role, such as local quarrymen who guarded the shafts of Box Tunnel. Due to the dearth of small arms, only a few civilians had rifles, so in fact they were watchmen rather than guards. In September 1914 guard companies were formed consisting of a major, or captain, two subalterns and 125 others to guard railways, docks and prisoner-of-war camps. In April 1916 they became the Royal Defence Corps.

The original weapon was a Martini-Enfield carbine with a short bayonet, later replaced by the long Ross rifle. However, the latter was a source of danger when a bayonet was fixed within the confined space of many sentry beats, and quite a number of soldiers received serious injuries when bayonets were struck by passing trains. Eventually an order was given that forbade soldiers carrying fixed bayonets at rail level. It was also a risky time for railway servants as they could be shot if they failed to answer a challenge quickly enough. To aid identification, railway employees carried a card or disc.

Initially these guards when off-duty were housed in waiting rooms, lamp rooms, porters' rooms and platelayers' huts. Later,

Soldiers guard a railway bridge at Little Somerford, Wiltshire, during the First World War.

old coach bodies were placed nearby, with all compartments removed except those at the two ends, one being left for the NCO in charge and the other used as a store room. A stove in the centre of the coach made for quite comfortable quarters. When the occupants realised that they were probably there for the duration of the war – they were generally older soldiers – they kept their surroundings spick and span and cultivated gardens.

Supplying them with food could be a problem. At first, providing coal was difficult until the guards asked enginemen to supply it. They responded liberally to this request and caused a number of soldiers to be seriously injured through being struck by lumps hurled from the footplate.

In the early days of the war, every yard of certain lines were patrolled day and night. Each patrol post had 3 to 4 miles of track and sent a patrol each way every two hours. They carried carbines slung, with no fixed bayonets, together with a red flag by day, and a light, normally white, at night, and twelve detonators. If an obstruction was found, they were required to run 400yd towards an approaching train, place two detonators on the track; return to the point of obstruction and fix two more detonators and then remain there holding a red flag, or a red light. Drivers complained of careless guards who had not been railwaymen displaying a red light when there was no danger, so red lamps were replaced by waved hurricane lamps.

Railway arches that had been let were subject to search and the antecedents of tenants investigated. Sometimes in order to bluff the enemy, guards on a certain line were doubled to encourage them to think it was to be used by troops for embarkation, when in fact no extra troop trains were run. In April 1916 almost all tunnel guards were dispensed with and in June 1917 almost all the remaining guards withdrawn. It was believed that the cost of these guards had been justified as no line of communication had suffered injury at the hands of enemy spies or sympathisers.

THE MOST EXPENSIVE THIRD-CLASS FARE

IN THE WORLD?

Pre-First World War fares per mile were generally 3*d* first class; 2*d* second class and 1*d* third class. The Isle of Wight railways terminated at St John's Road station, Ryde, 1¼ miles from the steamer landing stage, so an extension of the railway was highly desirable. It was an expensive venture, requiring a tunnel and about ½ mile of railway set on a pier. The Act of Parliament authorising this extension adopted the usual practice adopted when railway works of short length were extremely expensive and sanctioned fares of 1*s* 0*d* first class, 9*d* second and 6*d* third.

The line opened on 12 July 1880 but the tunnel was so wet that pumps had to be used to keep it dry. Interestingly, although the station, signal box and permanent way staff were employed jointly by the London & South Western and London, Brighton & South Coast Railways, the trains working over the line belonged to the Isle of Wight Railway and the Isle of Wight Central Railway. Furthermore, the Isle of Wight Railway coaches were mostly ex-Metropolitan Railway steam stock, while in the 1960s when the line was electrified, ex-London Transport tube cars were used.

WASTING PUBLIC MONEY

After the First World War the Disposals Board of the Ministry of Munitions advertised in the daily press for purchasers of complete ambulance trains stripped of ambulance fittings. The *Transport & Travel Monthly* commented:

> It would be interesting to learn to whom these advertisements were supposed to appeal, by the sapient officers who authorised their insertion. For modern bogie railway carriages in trains of 15 or 16 vehicles, there are but two or three possible buyers at prices above old iron and firewood value – the owning company, the smaller railways that purchase their rolling stock second hand from the bigger railways, and the Pullman Company.
>
> A letter giving particulars of the coaches, addressed to such likely buyers would have received attention, and presumably sales would have been affected – at no expense, as even the letters would have been franked 'O.H.M.S.' [On His Majesty's Service].
>
> The Disposals Board might have had a brilliant brainwave and enquired of the Minister of Housing as to whether he could use any of the carriages for temporary housing the homeless. Local hospitals might have had similar suggestions made to them.

RAILWAY BOOKSTALLS

Initially, porters ran station bookstalls as a perk and by 1839 two men and four children were selling newspapers on the platform at Liverpool Lime Street, but the first platform bookstall was opened by William Marshall at the London & Blackwall's Fenchurch Street station in 1841. His son, Horace, set up others in the Midlands and South Wales, while Walkley & Son held the bookstall contract on the Bristol & Exeter. Newspaper sales at other stations were either by local newsagents, or retired or disabled railwaymen. When the London & Birmingham became part of the London & North Western, its general manager, Captain Mark Huish, discovered that one disabled railwayman, Gibb, was making a profit of £1,200 on a bookstall with an annual rent of only £60. The contract for stalls on all the company's stations was then put out to tender and won by W.H. Smith & Son for £1,500. Gibb was given notice to leave on 1 November 1848, but refused to go and had to be forcibly ejected by the police.

NO NEED TO ADVERTISE

In the nineteenth century there was a dearth of railway advertising as competition for passenger traffic was not acute and railways were dignified and aloof in their dealings with the travelling public.

It was only in the twentieth century that railways sought patronage, perhaps the extension of the Great Central Railway to London in 1899 providing the necessary stimulation. As other railways already served London, the GCR needed to wheedle away passengers from those routes if it was to become viable. It advertised: 'Each express is vestibuled, and has a restaurant car available for first and third-class passengers' – in other words, all the latest features. The GCR stock, with its bogie coaches and on-board toilets, was quite a contrast to the East Coast stock of six-wheelers, or the third-class, non-corridor stock of the West Coast companies.

A 1922 advertisement encouraging people to live in the suburbs of north-west London – with the hope that they would patronise the Metropolitan Railway.

About the same time, the North Eastern Railway produced attractive Moorland coloured posters to attract holidaymakers to its area, while the Furness Railway's Lakeland posters performed similar aid to north-west England. The Great Western Railway produced tempting posters comparing the shape of Cornwall with Italy and implied that perhaps, rather than travel all that distance on the Continent, one should go to Cornwall instead.

To satisfy the growing number of those interested in railways, the London & North Western Railway produced postcards of its locomotives and rolling stock, selling over 7 million and thus making publicity pay, rather than having to be paid for. One of its excellent posters simply showed quadruple track near Whitmore with the caption 'The Best Permanent Way in the World'.

The Great Western Railway offered a prize for providing the best name for its new non-stop express to Cornwall. It also published a series of books; initially paperback guides sold for 3d such as *Smiling Somerset*, while later hardback books covered such features as castles, cathedrals and abbeys. The first issue of *Holiday Haunts* appeared in 1906, giving details of holiday places on the GWR system and addresses for accommodation. The first edition contained 538 pages, but by the 1930s this had risen to a chunky 1,000 or more pages.

In 1911 the GWR catered for railway enthusiasts by producing the *GWR Engine Book* with details of all its locomotives. This was followed by a series of highly readable books for 'boys of all ages' giving details of how the railway was run. Another means of bringing the line into the limelight was issuing a GWR board game and producing railway jigsaw puzzles. The GWR was also the pioneer of organised visits to the locomotive works.

The Lancashire & Yorkshire Railway produced a poster warning of the dangers of road, water and air transport compared with the safety of rail travel. The Metropolitan Railway adopted a different tack by enticing people to Metro-land in north-west London, where they could live in almost rural surroundings and travel daily – by the Metropolitan Railway, of course – to the City. The Great Northern Railway favoured humorous posters like the famous 'Skegness is so Bracing'.

UNFRIENDLY RAILWAYS

Railway companies were often unfriendly towards each other when striving to maximise profits. On 20 December 1866 the Salisbury & Dorset Junction Railway opened from Alderbury Junction, 4 miles south of Salisbury, to West Moors, thus providing a short cut to Poole and Weymouth. The new line was hardly a roaring success as the London & South Western Railway, which worked the line on behalf of the Salisbury & Dorset, was only able to hand over £14 to the Salisbury company in the first six months as its share of the takings.

Although receipts increased, the LSWR proved most obstructive and did its best to dissuade passengers from using the line, as it earned a higher income if passengers travelled the whole journey over the LSWR's own longer route. Ploys to deter passengers patronising the Salisbury & Dorset included using uncomfortable 'very old and very small carriages' on the branch trains it provided and ordering Waterloo booking clerks not to issue tickets via that route.

THE GREAT EASTERN RAILWAY
CREATES A STINK

The local sanitary authority of the Stratford district discovered that the waters of the never clear or limpid Channelsea and Lea had been further polluted by an oily iridescent matter with a pungent odour. When its inspectors began to seek its source, they discovered the waste products from the GER's oil-gas works at Stratford to be the cause.

The serving of a sanitary notice on the GER requiring an immediate end of the nuisance caused James Holden, the GER's locomotive superintendent, to experiment with the oil-gas waste and discovered it could become an oil fuel to replace coal in locomotives.

A WILTSHIRE STINK

Messrs Harris' factory at Calne produced pig products and a truck load of pigs' hair crawling with maggots was sent away each Saturday morning in an open wagon. Because of the horrible stench, the driver did not want it near his engine, nor the guard by his van.

On one occasion, for a joke, the Chippenham shunters put the wagon by the Down platform, close to the station master's office. Its offensive smell soon made its presence felt and the station master phoned through to the goods yard and asked them to remove it.

The wagon was usually placed on the Up side awaiting collection in the afternoon to Marsh & Baxter, Brierley Hill, Staffordshire, another part of the Harris' combine.

GEOMETRY PROBLEM

Following the Second World War Britain experienced a serious shortage of coal. One driver who lived in the suburbs of Bath and whose garden backed on to the railway believed he had the answer to the problem.

Before his engine passed his back garden, he would arrange for a large lump of coal to be on the footplate and then, quite accidentally of course, he would nudge it off so it would roll down the embankment, pass through the wire fence and into his garden.

In the event, the plan did not quite succeed. As anticipated, the lump of coal bounced down the embankment, went 'ping' through the fence, but he had got the angle wrong and it went into next door's garden. Furthermore, it punched a hole in next door's hen house.

When the gentleman next door found a lump of coal in his hen house and a hole in its wall, knowing of his neighbour's occupation he put two and two together, had a word with him and ordered him to repair the damage.

On hearing the above story from another engine driver, I thought it would interest one of my father's cousins who had lived in the same road as the coal-seeking engine driver. When I related the story to her she replied: 'It was my father's hen house' – in other words, the punctured hen house had belonged to the author's great uncle.

INDEX

Acton Bridge 167
Ahrons, E.L. 104
Aintree 176
Alderbury 219
Aldersgate 180
Aldgate 158
Alsopp & Sons 180
Arbroath 205
Ashburton 201
Ashton Gate 206
Aspinall, J. 91, 115
Avonwick 57
Axminster 44
Aylesbury 158, 203

Backwater 97
Baker Street 158
Balcombe 150
Bangour 196
Barlow, W.H. 22
Barmouth 102
Basingstoke 106,
   152, 179
Bass, Messrs 22, 180
Bath 12, 35, 108,
   171, 221
Bathampton 139
Beattock 50
Bentley 206
Bevois Park 193
Blackburn 78
Blackpool 43, 178–9
Blackwall 159
Blair Atholl 150
Blakeney 55
Blisworth 164
Botley 77
Bourne 10
Bovington 137
Box Tunnel 136, 213

Boxmoor 27
Brander 126
Brighton 129
Bristol 9, 12, 105, 190
Bristol Aeroplane
   Company 125
Brixham 208
Brunel, I.K. 12, 107,
   118, 136, 139
Burton 22, 180
Bury St Edmunds 189
Bury, E. 88, 113
Buxton 42

Caledonian Railway 62,
   70–1, 84, 91, 157
Calne 141, 220
Camden 88
Canterbury &
   Whitstable
   Railway 52
Carlisle 76
Catterick 153
Central London
   Railway 48
Charfield 171
Charing Cross 27,
   155, 180
Chedworth 170
Chesham 158
Chichester 142
Chiddy, J. 190
Chippenham 221
Christchurch 148
Church W. 78
Churchward, G.J. 61
Cliffe 33
Cooksbridge 121
Copmanthorpe 163
Coppenhall 72

Covent Garden 16
Cowlairs 63–5
Cramlington 63
Creech 147
Crewe 101
Cromford 133
Cruden Bay 177
Crystal Palace 198

Dartmouth 9
Davidson, Mr 83
Dean 109
Deechmont 197
Denton 15
Ditton 20
Doncaster 156
Dover 41, 183–4
Dovey 10
Droitwich 212
Dublin 63
Dullingham 182
Dundee 11

Eaglescliffe 25
Ealing 158
Earl's Court 201
Earswick 163
Ecclefechen 50
Edgware Road 180
Edinburgh 36, 63, 83
Ellis, G. 181
Ely 21
Eton 10, 194
Ettington 38
Euston 27, 109, 188
Exeter 14, 50, 124, 201

Fairlie 59
Falmouth 186
Fareham 77

Farleigh Down 117
Farringdon Street 136
Fenchurch Street 160, 217
Fife 9
Filton 125
First World War 17–19, 26, 40, 52–4, 63, 66, 68–70, 72, 95, 100, 115, 118, 120, 137, 152, 171, 188–9, 197, 204, 206, 210, 212–16
Flax Bourton 100
Fleetwood 35, 178
Folkestone 83, 151, 183
Foss Cross 170
Fowler, J. 94
Fulton, H.H. 116
Furness Railway 218

Gara Bridge 58
Garstang & Knott End 149
Georgetown 28
Gipsy Hill 198
Girvan 153
Gladstone, W.E. 91
Glasgow 63–5, 105, 167
Godalming 24
Gooch, D. 61, 94
Gosport 13, 111, 114
Great Central Railway 48, 123, 217
Great Eastern Railway 26, 189, 206, 210, 220
Great Malvern 212
Great Northern Railway 22, 53, 55, 89, 106–7, 145, 156, 166
Great Train Robbery 72
Great Western Railway 9–10, 23, 25, 29, 37, 46, 48, 57, 61–3, 68, 76, 78, 86, 89, 104, 109, 114, 120, 124, 136, 149, 156, 168, 170, 173, 184, 188, 194, 204, 218
Greenwich 92, 173
Grimsby 183
Guildford 132

Hadley 65
Hampstead 188
Hampton Court 119
Hanham 190
Harpenden 198
Hartlepool 11
Hatfield 106
Havant 199
Hayle 133
Haywards Heath 121
Hellingly 16
Hemel Hempstead 27, 198
Henley-in-Arden 184
Highland Railway 40, 67
Honiton 195
Hookham, J. A. 93
Hopton 133
Huddersfield 157
Hull 184
Hundred of Manhood & Selsey Tramway 142

Ilfracombe 209
Immingham 85
Invergordon 20

Kennington 172
Kentsford 197
Keymer 121
Keynsham 190
Killiecrankie 150
Kilnsea 33
Kincraig 20
King's Cross 32, 36, 136, 199
Kingswear 9
Kirtlebridge 71

Ladmanlow 133
Landore 107
Lane, A. 14
Lardner, Dr 136
Leicester Square 16
Leigh 65
Leighton 109
Lickey 153
Lindall 200
Linlithgo 37
Liskeard & Caradon 192
Liverpool & Manchester 11, 41

Liverpool Overhead 176
Livingstone 196
Llanelli 99, 162
Llansamlet 107
London & North Western Railway 20, 27, 55, 63, 70–1, 74–6, 80, 91, 99, 101–2, 109, 121, 137, 156, 167, 176, 188, 194, 203, 206, 217–19
London & South Western Railway 17, 23, 40, 44, 49, 52, 71, 77, 90, 100, 109, 119, 132, 137, 152, 168, 174, 182, 187, 192, 199, 209, 216, 220
London Bridge 46, 155, 159
London, Brighton & South Coast Railway 17, 68, 80, 89, 107, 156, 166, 187, 198, 216
London, Midland & Scottish Railway 164, 176
Ludgershall 57

McDonnell, A. 60
McIntosh, J. 62, 66
Manchester & Birmingham Railway 36
Manchester & Leeds Railway 35
Marsh, D.E. 89, 107
Martello 151
Marylebone 123
Masserano, C. 75
Maudland 35
Metropolitan Railway 94, 106, 135, 157–8, 188, 197, 216, 218–9
Middleton 133
Midland Railway 22, 27, 53, 72, 93, 133, 135, 169, 185, 188, 198–9
Milngavie 129
Minories 160

Monkton Combe 110
Muller, F. 38–9

Nailsea 174
Neath 32
Netley 18
Network Rail 124, 155
Newhaven 121
Newmarket 182, 203
Nine Elms 75, 100
North British Railway
    65, 81, 105, 185, 196
North Eastern Railway
    25, 67–8, 107, 116,
    118, 163, 218
North End 15
North London Railway
    38, 53
North Staffordshire
    Railway 93
Northallerton 67, 168

Paddington 61, 180, 186
Paignton 175
Palmer, H.R. 127
Patrington 32
Penzance 42, 124
Peterborough 108
Petersfield 130
Pevensey 11
Pinmore 154
Pole, F. 168
Port Carlisle 81
Portal, W. 77
Portishead 46, 105, 206
Portland 32, 40, 97
Portsmouth Arms 210
Preston 43, 130
Prosser, W. 132
Pudsey 22
Pwllyrhebog 85

Ramsey, J. 205
Red Hall 10
Redcar 15
Richborough 63, 137
Riches, T.H. 85
Rock, A.F. 93
Rodwell 97
Romford 66
Rugby 109
Runcorn 20

Rush, R.W. 144
Ryde 215

Salisbury 219
Seaforth 176
Second World War 19,
    40, 171, 181, 221
Sekon, G.A. 187
Selway, C.J. 179
Shanklin 42
Sheppey 53
Shipston 73
Silloth 185
Slamannan 37
Slough 10, 180, 194
Smith, W.H. 84, 217
Solway Viaduct 212
South Eastern &
    Chatham Railway 24,
    46, 53, 68, 103, 115,
    145, 150, 156, 159
Southall 120
Southampton 52, 157
Spurn 32–3
St Pancras 22–3, 26, 181
Stanlow & Thornton 15
Stephenson, G. 187
Stockton &
    Darlington 10
Stokes Bay 116
Stony Stratford 176
Stratford-upon-Avon
    & Midland Junction
    Railway 38
Strensall 163
Sugar Loaf 15
Surbiton 12
Swanwick 77
Sway 148
Swindon 101, 104,
    114, 150
Swindon, Marlborough
    & Andover
    Railway 59

Taff Vale 85
Tal-y-Lyn 167
Tavistock 40
Templecombe 50
Thayer, R.E. 92
Thingley 141
Thornbury 116

Thorne 131
Thornton 9
Tidworth 57
Tite, W. 13
Topsham 58
Torquay 208
Torrington 210
Tottenham Court
    Road 27
Travelling Post Office 50

Uphall 196

Victoria, Queen 10, 37,
    91, 117, 194
Victoria station 27, 41,
    54, 155, 184

Walker, H. 121
Watchet 197
Waterloo 19, 40, 43,
    49, 102, 119, 209
Watkin, E. 183
Webb, F.W. 80, 101, 194
Welbeck 32
West Hampstead 12
West Sussex
    Railway 144
Weymouth 40
Whale Island 186
Whaley Bridge 133
Wick 42
Wickwar Tunnel 97
Windsor 194
Winsford 72
Woking 37, 132
Wolferton 165
Wolvercote 131
Wolverhampton 88, 176
Woodchester 172
Woodfield 16
Woody Bay 118
Wool 137
Woolwich 95
Wootton Bassett 151
Worcester 211
Worksop 32

Yolland, Col 141
York 163